D0886555

DISCIPLINE IS DESTINY

DISCIPLINE
IS
DESTINY

THE POWER OF SELF-CONTROL

RYAN HOLIDAY

PORTFOLIO · PENGUIN

PORTFOLIO · PENGUIN
An imprint of Penguin Random House LLC
penguinrandomhouse.com

Copyright © 2022 by Ryan Holiday
Penguin Random House supports copyright. Copyright fuels creativity, encourages diverse voices, promotes free speech, and creates a vibrant culture. Thank you for buying an authorized edition of this book and for complying with copyright laws by not reproducing, scanning, or distributing any part of it in any form without permission. You are supporting writers and allowing Penguin Random House to continue to publish books for every reader.

Most Portfolio books are available at a discount when purchased in quantity for sales promotions or corporate use. Special editions, which include personalized covers, excerpts, and corporate imprints, can be created when purchased in large quantities. For more information, please call (212) 572-2232 or email specialmarkets@penguinrandomhouse.com. Your local bookstore can also assist with discounted bulk purchases using the Penguin Random House corporate Business-to-Business program. For assistance in locating a participating retailer, email B2B@penguinrandomhouse.com.

LIBRARY OF CONGRESS CATALOGING-IN-PUBLICATION DATA
Names: Holiday, Ryan, author.
Title: Discipline is destiny : the power of self-control / Ryan Holiday.
Description: New York, New York : Portfolio/Penguin, 2022.
Identifiers: LCCN 2022018989 (print) | LCCN 2022018990 (ebook) |
ISBN 9780593191699 (hardcover) | ISBN 9780593191705 (ebook)
Subjects: LCSH: Self-control. | Conduct of life. | Stoics.
Classification: LCC BJ1533.D49 H65 2022 (print) |
LCC BJ1533.D49 (ebook) | DDC 179/.9—dc23/eng/20220624
LC record available at https://lccn.loc.gov/2022018989
LC ebook record available at https://lccn.loc.gov/2022018990

Printed in the United States of America
1 3 5 7 9 10 8 6 4 2

Book design by Daniel Lagin

Two words should be taken to heart and obeyed when exerting ourselves for good and restraining ourselves from evil—words that will ensure a blameless and untroubled life: persist and resist.

EPICTETUS

CONTENTS

Part II: THE INNER DOMAIN
(THE TEMPERAMENT)

Part III: THE MAGISTERIAL (THE SOUL)

The Four Virtues

~

It was long ago now that Hercules came to the crossroads.

At a quiet intersection in the hills of Greece, in the shade of knobby pine trees, the great hero of Greek myth first met his destiny.

Where exactly it was or when, no one knows. We hear of this moment in the stories of Socrates. We can see it captured in the most beautiful art of the Renaissance. We can feel his budding energy, his strapping muscles, and his anguish in the classic Bach cantata. If John Adams had had his way in 1776, Hercules at the crossroads would have been immortalized on the official seal of the newly founded United States.

Because there, before the man's undying fame, before the twelve labors, before he changed the world, Hercules faced a crisis, one as life-changing and real as any of us have ever faced.

Where was he headed? Where was he trying to go? That's the point of the story. Alone, unknown, unsure, Hercules, like so many, did not know.

Where the road diverged lay a beautiful goddess who offered

him every temptation he could imagine. Adorned in finery, she promised him a life of ease. She swore he'd never taste want or unhappiness or fear or pain. Follow her, she said, and his every desire would be fulfilled.

On the other path stood a sterner goddess in a pure white robe. She made a quieter call. She promised no rewards except those that came as a result of hard work. It would be a long journey, she said. There would be sacrifice. There would be scary moments. But it was a journey fit for a god. It would make him the person his ancestors meant him to be.

Was this real? Did it really happen?

If it's only a legend, does it matter?

Yes, because this is a story about us.

About our dilemma. About our own crossroads.

For Hercules, the choice was between vice and virtue, the easy way and the hard way, the well-trod path and the road less traveled. We all face this choice.

Hesitating only for a second, Hercules chose the one that made all the difference.

He chose virtue. "Virtue" can seem old-fashioned. Yet virtue—*arete*—translates to something very simple and very timeless: Excellence. Moral. Physical. Mental.

In the ancient world, virtue was comprised of four key components.

Courage.

Temperance.

Justice.

Wisdom.

The "touchstones of goodness," the philosopher-king Marcus Aurelius called them. To millions, they're known as the cardinal virtues, four near-universal ideals adopted by Christianity and most of Western philosophy, but equally valued in Buddhism, Hinduism, and just about every other philosophy you can imagine. They're called "cardinal," C. S. Lewis pointed out, not because they come down from church authorities but because they originate from the Latin *cardo*, or hinge.

It's *pivotal* stuff. It's the stuff that the door to the good life hangs on.

They are also our topic for this book, and for this series.

Four books.* Four virtues.

One aim: to help you choose . . .

Courage, bravery, fortitude, honor, sacrifice . . .

Temperance, self-control, moderation, composure, balance . . .

Justice, fairness, service, fellowship, goodness, kindness . . .

Wisdom, knowledge, education, truth, self-reflection, peace . . .

These are the key to a life of honor, of glory, of *excellence* in every sense. Character traits that John Steinbeck perfectly described as "pleasant and desirable to [their] owner and makes him perform acts of which he can be proud and with which he can be pleased." But the *he* must be taken to mean all of humankind.

---

* This is book 2.

There was no feminine version of the word *virtus* in Rome. Virtue wasn't male or female, it just *was*.

It still is. It doesn't matter if you're a man or a woman. It doesn't matter if you're physically strong or painfully shy, a genius or of average intelligence. Virtue is a universal imperative.

The virtues are interrelated and inseparable, yet each is distinct from the others. Doing the right thing almost always takes courage, just as discipline is impossible without the wisdom to know what is worth choosing. What good is courage if not applied to justice? What good is wisdom if it doesn't make us more modest?

North, south, east, west—the four virtues are a kind of compass (there's a reason that the four points on a compass are called the "cardinal directions"). They guide us. They show us where we are and what is true.

Aristotle described virtue as a kind of craft, something to pursue just as one pursues the mastery of any profession or skill. "We become builders by building and we become harpists by playing the harp," he wrote. "Similarly, then, we become just by doing just actions, temperate by doing temperate actions, brave by doing brave actions."

Virtue is something we do.

It's something we choose.

Not once, for Hercules's crossroads was not a singular event. It's a daily challenge, one we face not once but constantly, repeatedly. Will we be selfish or selfless? Brave or afraid? Strong or weak? Wise or stupid? Will we cultivate a good habit or a bad one? Courage or cowardice? The bliss of ignorance or the challenge of a new idea?

Stay the same . . . or grow?

The easy way or the right way?

Introduction

~

Would you have a great empire? Rule over yourself.

PUBLILIUS SYRUS

We live in times of plenty and freedom that would have been unfathomable to even our most recent ancestors. An ordinary person in a developed nation has at their disposal luxuries and opportunities that all-powerful kings were once impotent to acquire. We are warm in the winter, cool in the summer, stuffed full far more often than hungry. We can go where we want. Do what we want. Believe what we want. With the snap of our fingers, pleasures and distractions appear.

Bored where you are? Travel.

Hate your job? Change it.

Crave it? Have it.

Think it? Say it.

Want it? Buy it.

Dream it? Chase it.

Nearly anything you want, whenever you want it, however you'd like it, it's yours.

This is our human right. As it should be.

And yet . . . what do we have to show for all this? Certainly not widespread flourishing. Empowered, unshackled, blessed beyond expectation—why are we so damn unhappy?

Because we mistake liberty for license. Freedom, as Eisenhower famously said, is actually only the *"opportunity for self-discipline."* Unless we'd rather be adrift, vulnerable, disordered, disconnected, we are responsible for ourselves. Technology, access, success, power, privilege—this is only a blessing when accompanied by the second of the cardinal virtues: self-restraint.

Temperantia.

Moderatio.

Enkrateia.

Sophrosyne.

Majjhimāpaṭipadā.

Zhongyong.

Wasat.

From Aristotle to Heraclitus, St. Thomas Aquinas to the Stoics, from *The Iliad* to the Bible, in Buddhism, in Confucianism, in Islam—the ancients had many words and many symbols for what amounts to a timeless law of the universe: We must keep ourselves in check or risk ruin. Or imbalance. Or dysfunction. Or dependency.

Of course, not everyone's problems are a result of plenty, but *everybody* benefits from self-discipline and self-control. Life is not fair. Gifts are not handed out evenly. And the reality of this inequity is that those of us coming from a disadvantage have to be even more disciplined to have a chance. They have to work harder, they have less room for error. Even those with fewer freedoms still face countless daily choices about which urges to indulge, what actions they'll take, what they'll accept or demand from themselves.

~

In this sense, we're all in the same boat: The fortunate as well as the unfortunate must figure out how to manage their emotions, abstain from what should be abstained from, choose what standards to observe. We must master ourselves unless we'd prefer to be mastered by someone or something else.

We can say that each of us has a higher and lower self, and that these two selves are in a constant battle with each other. The *can* versus the *should*. What we can get away with, and what's *best*. The side that can focus, and the side that is easily distracted. The side that strives and reaches, the side that stoops and compromises. The side that seeks balance, the side that loves chaos and excess.

The word for this inner battle to the ancients was *akrasia,* but it's really that same Herculean crossroads once again.

What will we choose?

Which side will win?

Who will you be?

THE ULTIMATE FORM OF GREATNESS

In the first book of this series on the cardinal virtues, courage was defined as the willingness to put your ass on the line—for something, for someone, for what you know you need to do. Self-discipline—the virtue of temperance—is even more important, the ability to keep your ass *in line.*

The ability . . .

. . . to work hard

. . . to say no

. . . to practice good habits and set boundaries

. . . to train and to prepare

. . . to ignore temptations and provocations

. . . to keep your emotions in check

. . . to endure painful difficulties.

Self-discipline is giving everything you have . . . and knowing what to hold back. Is there some contradiction in this? No, only *balance.* Some things we resist, some things we pursue; in all things, we proceed with moderation, intentionally, reasonably, without being consumed or carried away.

Temperance is not deprivation but command of oneself physically, mentally, spiritually—demanding the best of oneself, even when no one is looking, even when allowed less. It takes courage to live this way—not just because it's hard, but because it sets you apart.

Discipline, then, is both predictive and deterministic. It makes it more likely you'll be successful and it ensures, success or failure, that whatever happens, *you are great.* The converse is also true: a lack of discipline puts you in danger; it also colors who and what you are.

~

Let us go back to Eisenhower and his idea that freedom is the opportunity for self-discipline. Does his own life not prove this? He plodded through some thirty years of unglamorous military postings before earning the rank of general and had to watch, stateside, as his colleagues won medals and acclaim on the battlefield. In 1944, when he was appointed Supreme Commander of the Allied Forces in World War II, he suddenly controlled an army of some three million men, the tip of a war effort that ultimately involved more than fifty million people. There, at the head of an alliance of nations totaling upward of seven hundred million citizens, he discovered that far from being exempt from the rules, he had to be stricter with himself than ever. He came to find that the best way to lead was not by force or fiat, but through persuasion, through compromise, through patience, by controlling his temper, and, most of all, by example.

Emerging from the war, he was a victor of victors, having achieved conquest at a level no man-at-arms ever has or hopefully will ever again. Then, as president, overseeing a newfound arsenal of nuclear weapons, he was literally the most powerful human being in the world. There was almost no one or nothing that could tell him what to do, nothing that could stop him, no one who did not look up at him in admiration or away from him in fear. Yet his presidency involved no new wars, no use of those horrible weapons, no escalation of conflict, and he left office with prescient warnings about the machinery that creates war, the so-called military-industrial complex. Indeed, Eisenhower's most notable use of force in office came when he sent the 101st Airborne Division to protect a group of black children on their way to school for the first time.

And where were the scandals? Public enrichment? Broken promises?

There weren't any.

His greatness, like all true greatness, was not rooted in aggression or ego or his appetites or a vast fortune, but in simplicity and restraint—in how he commanded himself, which in turn made him worthy of commanding others. Contrast him with the conquerors of his time: Hitler. Mussolini. Stalin. Contrast him even with his contemporaries: MacArthur. Patton. Montgomery. Contrast him with his peers of the past: Alexander the Great. Xerxes. Napoleon. In the end, what endures, what we truly marvel at, is not the ambition but the self-mastery. The self-awareness. *The temperance.*

As a young man, Eisenhower's mother had quoted him a verse from the Book of Proverbs, "He that is slow to anger is better than the mighty," she had told him, "and he that ruleth his spirit than he that taketh a city." She taught him the same lesson that Seneca himself tried to instill in the rulers he advised, that "Most powerful is he who has himself in his own power."

And so it goes that Eisenhower quite literally conquered the world by conquering himself first.

Still, there is a part of us that celebrates, perhaps envies, those who let themselves get away with more, who hold themselves to lower standards—the rock stars, the famous, the wicked. It seems easier. It seems like more fun. It might even be the way to get ahead.

Is that right?

No, it is an illusion. Under closer inspection: No one has a harder time than the lazy. No one experiences more pain than the glutton. No success is shorter lived than the reckless or endlessly ambitious. Failing to realize your full potential is a terrible punishment. Greed moves the goalposts, preventing one from ever enjoying what one has. Even if the outside world celebrates them, on the inside there is only misery, self-loathing, and dependence.

With regards to temperance, the ancients were fond of the

metaphor of a charioteer. To win the race, one must not only get their horses to run quickly—but also keep the team under control, calm their nerves and jitters, have such a firm grasp on the reins that they can steer with pinpoint precision in even the most difficult of circumstances. The charioteer must figure out how to balance strictness and kindness, the light and the heavy touch. They have to pace themselves and their animals, and find every ounce of speed when it counts. A driver without control will go fast . . . but they will inevitably crash. Especially around the hairpin turns of the arena and the winding, pockmarked road of life. Especially when the crowd and the competition are rooting for exactly that.

It is through discipline that not only are all things possible, but also that all things are enhanced.

Name someone truly great without self-discipline. Name one calamitous undoing that was not, at least in part, rooted in a lack of self-discipline.

More than talent, life is about temperament. And temperance.

The people we admire most and will explore in this book— Marcus Aurelius, Queen Elizabeth II, Lou Gehrig, Angela Merkel, Martin Luther King Jr., George Washington, Winston Churchill—inspire us with their restraint and dedication. The cautionary tales of history—Napoleon, Alexander the Great, Julius Caesar, King George IV—stun us with their self-inflicted destruction. And because each of us contains multitudes, sometimes we see both excess and restraint in the same person and can learn from both.

Freedom requires discipline.

Discipline gives us freedom.

Freedom and greatness.

Your destiny is there.

Will you grab the reins?

DISCIPLINE IS DESTINY

PART I

THE EXTERIOR
(THE BODY)

Our body is our glory, our hazard and our care.

MARTHA GRAHAM

We begin with the self—the physical form. In St Paul's first letter to the Corinthians, we're told to keep under the body, and bring it into subjection, so that we will not be made a castaway. The Roman tradition, according to the Stoics, was about "endurance, a frugal diet, and a modest use of other material possessions." They wore functional clothes and shoes, ate off functional plates, drank moderately out of functional glasses, and committed earnestly to the rituals of ancient life. Do we pity this? Or admire its simplicity and dignity? In a world of abundance, each of us must wrestle with our desires, our urges, as well as the timeless battle to strengthen ourselves for the vicissitudes of life. This is not about six-pack abs or the avoidance of all that feels good, but instead about developing the fortitude required for the path we have chosen. It's about being able to go the distance, and steering clear of the blind alleys and mirages along the way. If we don't dominate ourselves physically, who and what does dominate? Outside forces. Laziness. Adversity. Entropy. Atrophy. We do the work, today and always, because it's what we're here for. And we know that while it might seem easy to take it easy and more pleasurable to indulge our pleasure centers, in the long run, it is a far more painful route.

Ruling Over the Body . . .

~

He played through fevers and migraines. He played through crippling back pain; pulled muscles; sprained ankles; and once, the day after being hit in the head by an eighty-mile-per-hour fastball, he suited up and played in Babe Ruth's hat, because the swelling made it impossible to put on his own.

For 2,130 consecutive games, Lou Gehrig played first base for the New York Yankees, a streak of physical stamina that stood for the next five-and-a-half decades. It was a feat of human endurance so long immortalized that it's easy to miss how incredible it actually was. The Major League Baseball regular season in those days was 152 games. Gehrig's Yankees went deep in the postseason, nearly every year, reaching the World Series a remarkable seven times. For seventeen years, Gehrig played from April to October, without rest, at the highest level imaginable. In the off-season, players barnstormed and played in exhibition games, sometimes traveling as far away as Japan to do so. During his time with the Yankees, Gehrig played some 350

2

doubleheaders and traveled at least two hundred thousand miles across the country, mostly by train and bus.

Yet he never missed a game.

Not because he was never injured or sick, but because he was an Iron Horse of a man who refused to quit, who pushed through pain and physical limits that others would have used as an excuse. At some point, Gehrig's hands were X-rayed, and stunned doctors found at least *seventeen* healed fractures. Over the course of his career, he'd broken nearly every one of his fingers—and it not only hadn't slowed him down, but he'd failed to say a word about it.

In another sense, he's almost unfairly famous for the streak, which overshadows the stats he accumulated along the way. His career batting average was an unbelievable .340, which he topped only when it counted, hitting .361 in his postseason career. (In two different World Series, *he batted over .500*.) He hit 495 home runs, including twenty-three grand slams—a record that stood for more than seven decades. In 1934, he became just the third player ever to win the MLB Triple Crown, leading the league in batting average, home runs, and RBIs (runs batted in). He's sixth all time with 1,995 RBIs, making him, effectively, one of the greatest teammates in the history of the game. He was a two-time MVP, seven-time All-Star, six-time World Series Champion, Hall of Famer, and the first player ever to have his number retired.

While the streak started in earnest in June 1925, when Gehrig replaced Wally Pipp, a Yankees legend, in reality, his Herculean endurance could be seen at an early age. Born to German immigrants in New York in 1903, Gehrig was the only one of four children to survive infancy. He entered the world a whopping fourteen pounds, and his mother's German cooking seems to have plumped him up from there. It was the teasing of school kids that first hardened the determination of the young boy, sending him to his father's *turnverein,* a German gymnastics club where Gehrig began to develop the powerful lower body that later drove in so many runs. Not naturally coordinated, a boyhood friend once joked that Gehrig's body often "behaved as if it were drunk."

He wasn't born an athlete. He made himself one.

Life as a poor immigrant was not easy. Gehrig's father was a drinker, and a bit of a layabout. It's more than ironic to read of his father's chronic excuses and sick days. This example shamed Gehrig, inspiring him to turn dependability and toughness into nonnegotiable assets (in a bit of foreshadowing, he never missed a day of school). Thankfully, his mother not only doted on him, she provided an incredible example of a quiet, indefatigable work ethic as well. She worked as a cook. She worked as a laundress. She worked as a baker. She worked as a cleaning lady, hoping to provide her son a ticket to a better life.

But the poverty, the poverty was always there. "No one who went to school with Lou," a classmate recalled, "can forget the cold winter days and Lou coming to school wearing [a] khaki shirt, khaki pants and heavy brown shoes, but no overcoat, nor any hat." He was a poor boy, a fate no one would choose, but it did shape him.

There is a story about Cleanthes, the Stoic philosopher, who, as he walked through Athens on a cold day, had his thin cloak blown open by a gust of wind. Observers were stunned to find he had little else on underneath, despite the frigid temperatures. Slowly, they burst into applause at the sheer endurance of it. So it went with Gehrig, who, even as his Yankees salary made him one of the highest-paid athletes in America, was rarely seen in a hat or even a vest in New York winters. Only later, when he married a kind and loving woman, could he be convinced to put on a coat—for her sake.

Most kids like to play sports. Lou Gehrig saw in the game a higher calling. Baseball was a profession that demanded control of, as well as care for, the body—since it was both the obstacle and the vehicle for success.

Gehrig did both.

He worked harder than anyone. "Fitness was almost a religion to him," one teammate would say of him. "I am a slave to baseball," Gehrig said. A willing slave, a slave who loved the job and remained forever grateful at just the opportunity to play.

This kind of dedication pays dividends. When Gehrig stepped up to the plate, he was communing with something divine. He stood, serenely, in a heavy wool uniform that no player today could perform in. He would sway, trading weight between his feet, settling into his batting stance. When he swung at a pitch, it was his enormous legs that did the work—sending the ball off his bat, deep, deep, out of the ballpark.

Some batters have a sweet spot; Gehrig could hit anywhere, off anyone. And when he did? He *ran*. For a guy who was teased for having "piano legs," it's pretty remarkable that Gehrig stole home plate more than a dozen times in his career. He wasn't all power. He was speed too. Hustle. Finesse.

There were players with more talent, with more personality, with more brilliance; but nobody outworked him, nobody cared more about conditioning, and nobody loved the game more.

When you love the work, you don't cheat it or the demands it asks of you. You respect even the most trivial aspects of the pursuit—he never threw his bat, or even flipped it. One of the only times he ever got in trouble with management was when they found out he was playing stickball in the streets of his old neighborhood with local kids, sometimes even after Yankees games. He just couldn't pass up the opportunity to play . . .

Still, there must have been so many days when he wasn't feeling it. When he wanted to quit. When he doubted himself. When it felt like he could barely move. When he was frustrated and tired of his own high standards. Gehrig was not superhuman—he had the same voice in his head that all of us do. He just cultivated the strength—made a habit—of not listening to it. Because once you start compromising, well, now *you're* compromised . . .

"I have the will to play," he said. "Baseball is hard work and the strain is tremendous. Sure, it's pleasurable, but it's tough." You'd think that everyone has that will to play, but of course, that's not true. Some of us get by on natural talent, hoping never to be tested. Others are dedicated *up to a point,* but they'll quit if it gets too hard. That was true then, as it is now, even at the elite level. A manager in Gehrig's time described it as an "age of alibis"—everyone was ready with an excuse. There was always a reason why they couldn't give their best, didn't have to hold the line, were showing up to camp less than prepared.

As a rookie, Joe DiMaggio once asked Gehrig who he thought was going to pitch for the opposing team, hoping perhaps, to hear it was someone easy to hit. "Never worry about that, Joe," Gehrig explained. "Just remember they always save the best for the Yankees." And by extension, he expected every member of the Yankees to bring their best with them too. That was the deal: To whom much is given, much is expected. The obligation of a champion is to act like a champion . . . while working as hard as somebody with something to prove.

Gehrig wasn't a drinker. He didn't chase girls or thrills or drive fast cars. He was no "good-time Charlie," he'd often say. At the same time, he made it clear, "I'm not a preacher and I'm not a saint." His biographer, Paul Gallico, who grew up in New

7

York City only a few years ahead of Gehrig wrote that the man's "clean living did not grow out of a smugness and prudery, a desire for personal sanctification. He had a stubborn, pushing ambition. He wanted something. He chose the most sensible and efficient route to getting it."

One doesn't take care of the body because to abuse it is a sin, but because if we abuse the temple, we insult our chances of success as much as any god. Gehrig was fully ready to admit that his discipline meant he missed out on a few pleasures. He also knew that those who live the fast or the easy life miss something too—they fail to fully realize their own potential. Discipline isn't deprivation . . . it brings rewards.

Still, Gehrig could have easily gone in a different direction. In the midst of an early career slump while playing in the minor leagues, Gehrig went out one night with some teammates and got so drunk that he was still boozed up at first pitch the next day. Somehow, he didn't just manage to play, but he played better than he had in months. He found, miraculously, that the nerves, the overthinking, had disappeared with a few nips from a bottle between innings.

It was a seasoned coach who noticed and sat Gehrig down. He'd seen this before. He knew the short-term benefits of the shortcut. He understood the need for release and for pleasure too. But he explained the long-term costs, and he spelled out the future Gehrig could expect if he didn't develop more sustainable coping mechanisms. That was the end of it, we're told, and "not because of any prissy notions of righteousness that it was evil or wrong to take a drink but because he had a driving, non-stop ambition to become a great and successful ball player. Anything that interfered with that ambition was poison to him."

It meant something to him to be a ballplayer, to be a Yankee, to be a first-generation American, to be someone who kids looked up to.

Gehrig, as it happened, continued to live with his parents for his first ten seasons, often taking the subway to the stadium. More than financially comfortable, he later owned a small house in New Rochelle. To Gehrig, money was at best a tool, at worst a temptation. As the Yankees reigned over the game, the team was treated to an upgraded dugout, with padded seats replacing the old Spartan bench. Gehrig was spotted by the team's manager tearing off a section. "I get tired of sitting on cushions," he said of the posh life of an athlete in his prime. "Cushions in my car, cushions on the chairs at home—every place I go they have cushions."

He knew that getting comfortable was the enemy, and that success is an endless series of invitations to get comfortable. It's easy to be disciplined when you have nothing. What about when you have everything? What about when you're so talented that you can get away with not giving everything?

The thing about Lou Gehrig is that he *chose* to be in control. This wasn't discipline enforced from above or by the team. His temperance was an interior force, emanating from deep within his soul. He chose it, despite the sacrifices, despite the fact that others allowed themselves to forgo such penance and got away with it. Despite the fact that it usually wasn't recognized—not until long after he was gone anyway.

Did you know that immediately after Ruth's legendary "called" home run that Lou Gehrig hit one too? Without any dramatic gestures either. Actually, it was his *second* of the game. Or that they have the same number of league batting titles? Or that Ruth struck out almost twice as many times as Gehrig? Lou not only kept his body in check in a way that Ruth didn't (Ruth ballooned to 240 pounds), but Gehrig checked his ego too. He was, a reporter would write, "unspoiled, without the remotest vestige of ego, vanity or conceit." The team always came first. Before even his own health. Let the headlines go to whomever wanted them.

Could he have done otherwise? Yes, but then again, also no. He could never have tolerated it in himself.

Even his trainer once complained, in jest, "If all ballplayers were like Gehrig, there wouldn't be any job for trainers on ball clubs." Gehrig did his own prep, took care of his own training— just as religiously in the off-season as well—and rarely needed rubdowns or rehab. The only thing he asked of the staff was that a stick of gum be put out for him in his locker before a game, two if they were going into a doubleheader. Gehrig wore his fame lightly, an observer once noted, but took the obligations of it seriously.

But sports is more than just muscle and talent. Nobody plays that many games in a row without being a tough son of a bitch. A bad throw from his third baseman forced Gehrig to grab for the ball in the dirt, where he jammed his thumb into the ground. In the dugout, his teammate thought he'd be in for a cursing out. "I think it's broken," was all Gehrig said. "You didn't hear a peep out of Lou," the teammate recounted in amazement. "Never a word of complaint about my rotten throw and what it did to his thumb." And of course, he was back in the lineup the following day.

"I guess the streak's over," a pitcher joked after knocking Gehrig unconscious with a pitch in June 1934. For five terrible minutes, he lay there, unmoving, dead to the world—death being a real possibility in the era before helmets. He was rushed to the hospital, and most expected he'd be out for two weeks even if the X-ray for a skull fracture came back negative. Again, he was back in the batter's box the next day.

Still, you might have expected a hesitation, a flinch when the next ball came hurtling toward him. That's why pitchers will bean a batter from time to time—because it makes them cautious, the batter's instinct for self-preservation causes them to step back, in a game where a millimeter may make all the difference. Instead, Gehrig leaned in . . . and hit a triple. A few innings later, he hit another. And before the game was rained out, he hit his third . . . while recovering from a nearly fatal blow to the brain. "A thing like that can't stop us Dutchmen," was his only postgame comment.

What propels a person to push themselves this way? Sometimes, it's simply to remind the body who is in charge. "It's just that I had to prove myself right away," he said. "I wanted to make sure that big whack on my head hadn't made me gun-shy at the plate."

Gehrig may not have been after personal sanctification, but the truth was that he achieved it anyway. "There was no finer man that walked the Earth," one of his teammates observed. "He didn't drink, chew or smoke. And he was in bed by nine thirty or ten each night." Perfectly reachable habits, and yet it earned him incredible respect. Why? "When a man can control his life, his physical needs, his lower self," Muhammad Ali would later say, "he elevates himself."

There's an old story about Gehrig's first game with the Yankees, when he started his streak. He was supposedly hit with a ball that day too. "Do you want us to take you out?" the manager asked. "Hell no!" Gehrig was said to have exclaimed. "It's taken me three years to get into this game. It's going to take more than a crack on the head to get me out."

Seventeen years later, something finally did take him out and it was far more serious than a wild pitch. For someone who had so long been used to being in control, it must have been bewildering to Gehrig when his body stopped responding as it always had. Slowly but noticeably, his swing wasn't as fast. He struggled to pull on his mitt. He fell down while putting on a pair of pants. He dragged his feet when he walked. Yet his sheer will kept him together to a degree that few suspected anything was wrong. For a while, he fooled even himself.

Just a sample of Gehrig's schedule in August 1938: The Yankees played thirty-six games in thirty-five days. Ten games were doubleheaders; in one case, there were five consecutive days of them. He traveled to five cities, covering thousands of miles by train. He hit .329 with nine home runs and thirty-eight RBIs.

For an athlete to do this without missing a game, without missing an inning, in their midthirties, is impressive. But Lou Gehrig did it as the early stages of ALS ravaged his body, slowing his motor skills, weakening his muscles, and cramping his hands and feet.

It would be nearly a full additional season before Gehrig's body fully gave out. The streak had taken on a life of its own. It kept going, Gehrig gutting out hits and runs, despite the occasional but uncharacteristic error on the field.

But a man who knows his body, even as they push and push and push past their limitations, also has to know when to stop.

"Joe," he said to the Yankees manager on an ordinary May day in 1939. "I always said that when I felt I couldn't help the team anymore I would take myself out of the lineup. I guess that time has come."

"When do you want to quit, Lou?" McCarthy replied. *Quit.* That horrible word burned. His manager, still thinking they were talking about some date in the future, hoped they'd have more time together. But his body was too far gone. "Now," Gehrig replied with certainty. "Put Babe Dahlgren in."

What had changed? After weeks of inconsistent play, Gehrig had fielded a ground ball and made a solid out. It was a play he'd made thousands of times in his career. But his teammates had celebrated like it was one of his Series-winning homers. In that moment, he knew. He was holding them back. He was lying to himself.

It was Churchill who told the young boys at Harrow School to "Never give in, never give in, never, never, never, never—in nothing, great or small, large or petty . . . Never yield to force; never yield to the apparently overwhelming might of the enemy." For all his life, Gehrig had resisted in similar fashion. Poverty hadn't held him back. Nor had injuries or the sheer odds of making it in professional sports. He had resisted temptation, he had refused to give in to complacency or even fatigue. And yet here he was at one of the two exceptions that Churchill would lay out—"never give in except to convictions of honour and good sense"—now, at the end of the road, all Gehrig could do was exit with the same poise and control he had played with.

The streak that began back in the heady days of the Roaring Twenties, soldiered on through the Great Depression, and peaked with the 1938 World Series ended as inauspiciously as it began. Somebody new was getting their shot at first base. It came as a complete surprise to Dahlgren, his replacement. He was stepping into very big shoes. "Good luck," was all Gehrig could say.

As the starting lineup was called over the loudspeakers to some twelve thousand people in Detroit, the announcer was just as stunned. For the first time in 2,130 games, Gehrig's name was not to be called. Still, the announcer couldn't help himself, "How about a hand for Lou Gehrig, who played 2,130 games in a row before he benched himself today." The crowd, which included a friend of Gehrig's in town on business—the one and only Wally Pipp, whom Gehrig had first replaced fourteen years earlier—struggled to register what it meant. Then the crowd broke out in a sustained applause.

Gehrig waved and retreated to the dugout. His teammates watched in silence as the Iron Horse broke down and wept.

You have to do your best while you still have a chance. Life is short. You never know when the game, when your body, will be taken away from you. Don't waste it!

On July 4, 1939, he entered Yankee stadium for the final time in uniform. Stripped now of the muscles that had long served him, all that was left was the man himself, his courage and his self-mastery. Yet, it was in another sense, the same old battle against his body as it ever was—the battle against fatigue, the battle to push himself. He tried to beg off speaking, but the crowd chanted, "We want Lou! We want Lou!" Struggling to hold himself off, the words he would utter would prove Ali's point—that when we master the lower self, we elevate ourselves to a higher plane. "For the past two weeks you have been reading about a bad break," he said as he tried to keep himself together. "Yet today I consider myself the luckiest man on the face of the earth."

But eventually this luck would run out, as it does for us all.

"Death came to the erstwhile 'Iron Man' at 10:10 o'clock," the *New York Times* wrote in 1941. "The record book is liberally strewn with his feats at the plate." Yet it was not what was written about him, in the record books or elsewhere, that truly captured his legacy.

The funeral lasted just eight minutes. Looking out over the man's friends and teammates, the priest found a flowery eulogy unnecessary. "We need none," the preacher said of the man, "because you all knew him." No tribute was needed, his life, his example, spoke for itself.

Like Lou Gehrig, each of us is in a battle with our physical form. First, to master it and bring it to its full potential. Second, as we age or get sick, to arrest its decline—to quite literally wrest the life from it while we can. The body, you must understand, is a metaphor. It's a training ground, a proving ground for the mind and the soul.

What are you willing to put up with?

What can you do without?

What will you put yourself through?

What can you produce with it?

You say you love what you do. Where's your proof? What kind of streak do you have to show for it?

Most of us don't have millions of fans watching. Or millions of dollars incentivizing us. We don't have a coach or a trainer monitoring daily progress. There is no fighting weight for our profession. This actually makes our jobs, our lives harder—because we have to be our own manager, our own master. We're responsible for our own conditioning. We have to monitor our own intake, decide our own standards.

Good.

The truly dedicated are harder on themselves than any outside person could ever be. *Temperance* is not a particularly sexy word and hardly the most fun concept, but it can lead to greatness.

Temperance, like a tempered sword. Simplicity and modesty. Fortitude and self-control in all things—except our determination and toughness.

We owe it to ourselves, to our goals, to the game, to keep going. To keep pushing. To stay pure. To be tough.

To conquer our bodies before they conquer us.

Attack the Dawn

~

It was early, always early, when Toni Morrison awoke to write. In the dark, she would move quietly, making that first cup of coffee. She'd sit at her desk in her small apartment, and as her mind cleared and the sun rose and the light filled the room, she would write. She did this for *years*, practicing this secular ritual used not just by writers but by countless busy and driven people for all time.

"Writers all devise ways to approach that place where they expect to make the contact," she'd later reflect, "where they become the conduit, or where they engage in this mysterious process. For me, light is the signal in the transition. It's not being *in* the light, it's being there *before it arrives*. It enables me, in some sense."

But of course, it was as practical as it was spiritual. Because at the beginning of her career, Morrison was also a single working mother of two young boys. Her job as an editor for Random House occupied her days, her children every other minute, and by the late evening she was burned out, too tired to think. It was the precious early morning hours between the parting dark and the rising dawn, before her boys uttered the word *Mama*, before the pile of manuscripts from work demanded her attention, before the commute, before the phone calls, before the bills beckoned, before the dishes needed to be done, it was then that she could be a writer.

Early, she was free. Early, she was confident and clearheaded and full of energy. Early, the obligations of life existed only in theory and not in fact. All that mattered, all that was there, was the story—the inspiration and the art.

There she was, starting her first novel in 1965, freshly divorced, thirty-four years old and struggling as one of the few black women in an incredibly white, male industry. Yet in her mind, this was "the height of life." She was no longer a child, and yet for all her responsibilities, everything was quite simple: Her kids needed her to be an adult. So did her unfinished novel.

Wake up.

Show up.

Be present.

Give it everything you've got.

Which she did. Even after *The Bluest Eye* was published to rave reviews in 1970. She followed it with ten more novels, nine nonfiction works, five children's books, two plays, and short stories. And she earned herself a National Book Award, a Nobel Prize, and a Presidential Medal. Yet for all the plaudits, she must have been most proud of having done it *while* being a great mother, a great *working* mother.

Of course, it's not exactly fun to wake up early. Even the people who have reaped a lifetime of benefits from it, still struggle with it. You think you're not a morning person? *Nobody is a morning person.**

But at least in the morning, we are free. Hemingway would talk about how he'd get up early because there was "no one to disturb you and it is cool or cold and you come to your work and warm as you write." Morrison found she was just more confident in the morning, before the day had exacted its toll and the mind was fresh. Like most of us, she realized she was just "not very bright or very witty or very inventive after the sun goes down." Who can be? After a day of banal conversations, frustrations, mistakes, and exhaustion.

Not that it's all about being clever. There's a reason CEOs hit the gym early—they still have willpower then. There's a reason people read and think in the morning—they know they might not get time later. There's a reason coaches get to the facility before everyone else—they can get a jump on the competition that way.

Be up and doing.

While you're fresh. While you can. Grab that hour before

---

*While we might say that waking up early might not be for absolutely everyone . . . it is for *almost* everyone.

daylight. Grab that hour before traffic. Grab it while no one is looking, while everyone else is still asleep.

In Marcus Aurelius's *Meditations*, we hear the most powerful man in the world trying to convince himself to get out of bed at dawn when the lower part of himself wants desperately to stay. "Is *this* what I was created for?" he asks of his reluctance. "To huddle under the blankets and stay warm?"

Yes, it is nicer under there. But is that what we were born for? To feel nice? That's how you're going to spend the gift of life, the gift of this present moment that you will never have again? "Don't you see the plants, the birds, the ants, and the spiders and the bees going about their individual tasks, putting the world in order, as best they can?" he said to himself but also to us. "And you're not willing to do your job as a human being? Why aren't you running to do what your nature demands?"

Yet here we are, thousands of years later, still hitting the snooze button on our alarms. Here we are, wasting the most productive hours of the day, choosing to reject these moments before the interruptions, before the distractions, before the rest of the world gets up and going too. Passing on the opportunity to gather our flowering potential while it's freshest, still shining with morning dew.

"I think Christ has recommended rising early in the morning, by rising from his grave very early," observed the theologian Jonathan Edwards in the 1720s. Is that why quiet mornings seem so holy? Perhaps it's that we're tapping into the traditions of our ancestors, who also rose early to pray, to farm, to fetch water from the river or the well, to travel across the desert before the sun got too hot.

When you have trouble waking up, when you find it hard, remind yourself of who you come from, remind yourself of the tradition, remind yourself of what is at stake. Think, as Morrison did, of her grandmother, who had more children and an even harder life. Think of Morrison herself, who certainly did not have it easy, and still got up early.

Think of how lucky you are. Be glad to be awake (because it's better than the alternative, which we'll all greet one day). Feel the joy of being able to do what you love.

Cherish the time. But most of all, *use* it.

The Strenuous Life Is the Best Life

King George IV was a notorious glutton. His breakfast consisted of two pigeons, three steaks, a near full bottle of wine, and a glass of brandy. In time, he grew so fat he could no longer sleep lying down or the weight of his own chest might asphyxiate him. He had trouble signing documents—he eventually had his attendants make a stamp for his signature to save him even this basic exertion. Still, he managed to father several illegitimate children while generally neglecting the business of being a king.

King George was the type of person who apparently believed that he was exempt from the rules of health and humankind. That his body could and would endure unlimited abuse without consequence. Indeed, his last words, when years of bad habits and lethargy finally caught up with him at 3:30 AM in the summer of 1830, were:

"Good God, what is this?"

Then he realized what it was.

"My boy," he said as he grasped the hand of a page, "this is death."

It was almost as if he was surprised to find out that he was mortal . . . and that treating his body like a garbage can for four decades had consequences.

Has anyone ever drunk or eaten their way to happiness?

No.

An early grave? Misery? Regret?

You bet.

Take a look at the diet of Babe Ruth, as he played alongside Lou Gehrig. Breakfast was a pint of whiskey mixed with ginger ale, then steak, four eggs, fried potatoes, and a pot of coffee. For an afternoon snack, it was four hot dogs, each washed down with a bottle of Coca-Cola. He had an early supper and a late supper, each the same: two porterhouse steaks, two heads of lettuce drenched with blue cheese dressing, two platefuls of cottage-fried potatoes, and then two apple pies. Oh and between the two suppers, he had four more hot dogs and four more bottles of Coca-Cola.

Perhaps all that needs to be said is that Ruth was once rushed to the hospital for *drinking too much soda and eating too many hot dogs.*

It was fun while it went down, but the aftertaste was bitter.

"Listen, Lou," Babe once told Gehrig. "Don't be a sap. Keep in condition. Don't let yourself get soft. I made a lot of mistakes when I was coming along. I didn't eat right, and I didn't live right. Later I had to pay for all those mistakes. I don't want you to do the same thing."

Babe Ruth's athletic feats then, as inspiring as they are, carry with them a tinge of sadness. What could Babe Ruth have accomplished had he been more disciplined? What greatness did he leave on the table? Because yes, even the greats could have been greater.

The pleasure of excess is always fleeting. Which is why self-discipline is not a rejection of pleasure but a way to embrace it. Treating our body well, moderating our desires, working hard, exercising, hustling—this is not a punishment. This is simply the work for which pleasure is the reward.

Let's contrast King George with another head of state, President Theodore Roosevelt. Now, if anyone had an excuse for a sedentary existence, it was Teddy. He was born a weak and vulnerable boy. His interests were academic. The only thing worse than his very nearsighted eyes were his lungs, which seemed to rebel at the slightest bit of stress.

"Don't scold me," he once told his father, "or I shall have the asthma."

And on many nights he did. Crippling, terrifying attacks that nearly killed him.

But at his father's patient encouragement, Teddy began working out. Starting at a gym down the street, and then a gym on the family's porch, and later at Harvard, Theodore not only remade his body but remade his life and, in a sense, the world. *The strenuous life,* he would call it, a life of action, activity, but most of all, of exercise.

Walking. Rowing. Boxing. Wrestling. Hiking. Hunting. Horseback riding. Football. Roosevelt did it all. There was hardly a day when he was not actively exercising, playing sports, or getting out into nature. Even as president, he was active enough to put much younger people to shame. "While in the White House," Roosevelt wrote, "I always tried to get a couple of hours' exercise in the afternoons."

A couple hours a day! As president!

Who do you think felt better when they woke up in the morning? The lazy King George, whose life was all about pleasure? Or the occasionally sore Theodore Roosevelt, who chose the "strenuous life"—playing tennis or talking cold swims in Rock Creek or the Potomac? Even when he was injured (for instance, he lost sight in one eye from a boxing incident while president), he was having the better time!

And what do you think Teddy would have thought of our sedentary, digital lives? Or our excuse that we're too busy or too tired?

We are meant for more than simply existing. We are here for more than just lying around and seeking pleasure. We have been given incredible gifts by nature. We are an apex predator, a freakishly elite product of millions of years of evolution. How will you choose to spend this bounty? By letting your assets atrophy?

This isn't just a personal choice. It affects us all.

Nearly half of young Americans are actually ineligible to join the US military for health or fitness reasons. Intemperance is not a joke. Gluttony isn't good. This isn't just an existential issue, but a national security one.

If greatness is our aim, if we want to be productive, courageous members of society, we need to take care of our bodies. Not just in the gym, but in the kitchen too. A healthy diet, and not abusing drugs or drink, does much of the heavy lifting. You are a high-end race car. Fuel accordingly.

"Obviously the philosopher's body should be well prepared for physical activity," the Stoic Musonius Rufus explained, "because often the virtues make use of this as a necessary instrument for the affairs of life. We use the training common to both when we discipline ourselves to cold, heat, thirst, hunger, meager rations, hard beds, avoidance of pleasures and patience under suffering. For by these things . . . the body is strengthened and becomes capable of enduring hardship, study and ready for any task."

Life is filled with all sorts of difficulties and challenges. Work will not always go well. But working out? Working out is in our control. It is a contained space in which the only potential obstacle is our determination and commitment.

Swim. Lift weights. Train in jujitsu. Take long walks. You can choose the means, but the method is a must: You must be active. Get your daily win. Treat the body rigorously, as Seneca tells us, so that it may not be disobedient to the mind. Because as you're building muscle, you're also building willpower. More important, you're building this willpower and strength while most people are not.

Don't you think there were moments in the middle of the Coal Strike of 1902 when Teddy got tired? Don't you think it was exhausting to battle the trusts and their lawyers and their agents in the press? Can you imagine how he felt when that assassin's bullet pierced his chest moments before a speech?

Yeah, he wanted to quit. Yeah, he knew he was approaching his limits. Yeah, he knew that he *could* do less, that other leaders certainly felt obligated to do less. But he would never have accepted that in himself.

He kept going. He had experience with this. He knew that little voice in his head, the voice of fatigue and weakness, did not always need to be heeded.

He had trained for this.

He knew what he was capable of.

He had made his body, and now he could make it do what needed to be done.

Quit Being a Slave

~

He had landed at Normandy.

He had beaten the Nazis and occupied Germany.

He had published his memoirs and made a fortune.

In 1949, all that was left was to conquer himself.

So after a lifetime of battles, in a lifetime of battles of will, Dwight Eisenhower gave himself the order.

Quit smoking.

And just like that, he went to battle with a thirty-eight-year habit. In the scope of his life, this may not seem like much, but every addict knows that it can be harder to conquer an inner demon than any external enemy. "Few figures in public life have had Dwight D. Eisenhower's willpower," the biographer Jean Edward Smith wrote. "A lifetime smoker of three to four packs of cigarettes a day, Eisenhower quit cold turkey . . . and never touched a cigarette again."

"The only way to stop is to stop," he would tell an aide, "and I stopped." No one "made him,"—no one could have—but he saw it as his duty to enforce it on himself. It would add years to his life. And by protecting and mastering his body, it allowed him to be of service to the world, first leading NATO and then assuming the American presidency, in a fraught and tense period.

But what about you?

What are you hooked on? What do you have trouble doing without?

On an ordinary afternoon in 1949—the same year Eisenhower quit smoking—the physicist Richard Feynman was going about his business when he felt the pull to have a drink. Not an intense craving by any means, but it was a disconcerting desire for alcohol, completely divorced from the pleasure one earns as a reward for hard work. On the spot, Feynman gave up drinking right then and there. Nothing, he felt, should have that kind of power over him.

He wanted to quit before he got to that place where we kick ourselves, as the lyrics go . . .

Never again
Is what you swore
The time before

At the core of this idea of self-mastery is an instinctive reaction against anything that masters us. Who can be free when they have lost, as one addiction specialist put it, "the freedom to abstain"?

We say that we're after autonomy, and yet we willingly hand ourselves over to habits that tell us . . . more of *me* is all you need. That tell us we'll be unhappy, hungry, lonely, in pain, weak, without them.

How pathetic is that?

"Show me a man who isn't a slave," Seneca demanded, pointing out that even slave owners were chained to the responsibilities of the institution of slavery. "One is a slave to sex, another to money, another to ambition; all are slaves to hope or fear." The first step, he said, was to pull yourself out of the ignorance of your dependency, whatever it happens to be. Then you need to get clean—get clean from your mistress, from your addiction to work, from your lust for power, whatever. In the modern era, we might be hooked on cigarettes or soda, likes on social media, or watching cable news. It doesn't matter whether it's socially acceptable or not, what matters is whether it's good for you. Eisenhower's habit was killing him, as so many of ours are too—slowly, imperceptibly.

But even if they weren't, even if they were harmless, why should we take orders from our belly or our crotches . . . or the device that seems almost physically connected to us at this point? The body can't be in charge. Neither can the habit.

We must be the boss.

In some ways, the habit itself is less important than what we're really quitting, which is dependency. What the Buddhists call *tanha*. The *thirst*. The *craving*. Maybe with time you can go back to recreational usage—of whatever it is—yet even to do that, you're first going to have to quit the habituation. It's not the sex or the likes or the drink. It's the *need*. And it's this need that is the source of suffering.

Whether it's Amy Winehouse destroyed by drugs or Tiger Woods undone by his mistresses, the world grieves the many talented hosts destroyed by the parasite within them, the one that needed to be fed and fed and fed but was never full. The cost is not just personal but shared by us all, in symphonies never written, feats never accomplished, in good never done, the potential of an ordinary day never fulfilled.

Slavery, we have to remember, was a deeply inefficient and inferior economic system, on top of its misery and cruelty. Why would you choose to be one?! Especially to something that increasingly feels less good to do?

Here is an illuminating test: If it was invented today, would you start it? If alcohol was introduced to you now, for the first time, with all its determinants and risks known, would you still take a drink? Knowing how much time you spend on it now, would you still download that app if it launched today? If you knew the promotion and the success would leave you divorced and unhappy despite your riches, would you still have set out for it all those years ago? But just because you started, doesn't mean you have to continue. The fact that you didn't know then doesn't change the fact that you're *choosing* it now.

Everyone has coping mechanisms, things that take the edge

off . . . but soon enough, in enough quantities, they end up dulling our edge altogether. These things might comfort us, but they are not our friends. That's what Lou Gehrig's coach was trying to tell him when he caught Lou taking a nip before games for his nerves. *You're not going to like where this road ends,* he was saying. *And it always seems to end in the same place.*

Whatever the bad habit is, whatever seems to be ruling your life—socially acceptable or not—you have to quit. Whether it's cold turkey or with help, you've got to get off the stuff—whatever it is.

Everyone, no matter how powerful, has some bad habit they're wrestling with, but also that it's never too late to come back and beat it.

Eisenhower was fifty-eight years old. His habit itself was nearly middle-aged.

That doesn't matter. What counts is what we do about it today.

That we choose to stop being a slave.

We choose freedom.

We save ourselves so we can save (and keep saving) the world.

Avoid the Superfluous

~

Cato the Elder never wore a garment that cost more than a few dollars. He drank the same wine as his slaves, with whom he regularly worked alongside in the fields. He bought his food in the public markets. He rejected the expensive trappings of high society.

"Nothing is cheap," he said, "if it is superfluous."

If he didn't need it, he didn't buy it . . . if he didn't care about it, he didn't care if everyone else did. But the point of this frugality was not deprivation, it was independence. Cato lived in a modest home, inspired by one of his heroes, Manius Curius. At the height of the great conqueror's powers, some men were sent to bribe Curius but found him in his kitchen boiling turnips. In an instant, they knew their mission was futile. A man satisfied with so little could never be tempted.

When we desire more than we need, we make ourselves vulnerable. When we overextend ourselves, when we *chase,* we are not self-sufficient. This is why Cato declined expensive gifts, why he did his political work for no pay, why he traveled with few servants and kept things simple.

A Spartan king was once asked what the Spartans got from their "spartan" habits. "Freedom is what we reap from this way of life," he told him.

The boxer Rubin Carter survived some nineteen years of wrongful imprisonment. How? It wasn't his wealth that got him through but the opposite. He stripped himself, deliberately, of the most basic amenities in prison: no pillows, no radio, no rugs, no TV, no porn. Why? So that nothing could be taken from him. So that the guards had no leverage over him.

By being a little hard on ourselves, it makes it harder for others to be hard on us. By being strict with ourselves, we take away others' power over us.

A person who lives below their means has far more latitude than a person who can't. That's why Michelangelo, the artist, didn't live as austerely as Cato but he avoided the gifts dangled by his wealthy patrons. He didn't want to owe anyone. Real wealth, he understood, was autonomy.

It can seem like the life of a Cato or a Michelangelo is difficult, but in many ways, it's easier. Less to worry about. Fewer rings to kiss. Nothing to envy . . . or fear the envious will take from you.

Remember: No one is having less fun than an overextended, overcommitted person with debtors at their door . . . or a high-paying job they can't afford to lose. No one is less free than the person trapped on the treadmill moving faster and faster and faster but going nowhere.

I would *die* without my [insert luxury item], we'll say in jest. *How can anybody live like this?* we'll ask not so rhetorically.

The answer? They're stronger than you.

"The more a man is," the editor Maxwell Perkins had inscribed on his mantel, "the less he wants." When you strip away the unnecessary and the excessive, what's left is you. What's left is what's important.

How do you know if something is superfluous? Well, one indication can be how hard *other people* are pushing it on you. The insecure constantly pressure us to be like them. Another is how much your interest is motivated by *keeping up* or a *fear of missing out.* Ask yourself: Haven't I and humanity survived quite a long time without this? How did it go last time I got the thing I craved—how long did the feeling last (compared to the buyer's remorse)? And how will you know that this thing won't actually make your life easier? Because the last thing didn't either! Go check your junk drawer or the back of your closet for proof.

Think about how content you were with less just a few years ago. How much more frugal you were . . . by necessity. How much less you got by on. Do you look back at those younger years, when you were striving and struggling, as somehow lacking? As something you're bitter about?

Not usually. These were happy days. We almost miss them.

Things were simpler then. Cleaner. There was more clarity. Most of the luxuries that lay in the future we didn't even know about. We didn't pine for them. We were ignorant even of their possibility!

What it will do is make you less free, more dependent.

The less you desire, the richer you are, the freer you are, the more powerful you are.

It's that simple.

Clean Up Your Desk

⁓

Robert Moses was not a kind man, but he was effective. He got more done in his decades in power than few believed possible, building 2,567,256 acres of parkland, 658 playgrounds, 416 miles of parkways, 13 bridges, housing, tunnels, stadiums, civic centers, exhibition halls—some $27 billion in total of constructed public works across New York. He didn't just do his job well, he did multiple jobs well, simultaneously serving in twelve positions, including as New York City Parks Commissioner, president of the State Power Commission, and chairman of the Triborough Bridge and Tunnel Authority over a forty-four-year career.

Drive across the West Side Highway, that's Robert Moses. Cross the Harlem River on the Triborough Bridge—Robert Moses. Go to Niagara Falls State Park—Robert Moses. Visit Jones Beach—Robert Moses. Swim in the Astoria Pool—Robert Moses. The 1964–65 New York World's Fair—Robert Moses.

CLEAN UP YOUR DESK ☆ *DISCIPLINE IS DESTINY*

Central Park Zoo, Shea Stadium, Brooklyn–Battery Tunnel, Jones Beach Theater, Lincoln Center—Robert Moses.

His accomplishments that shaped and defined New York City from 1924 to 1968 deserve to be measured, his biographer said, not against his predecessors and successors, or even against other cities, but against *entire civilizations.*

How did he do it?

Raw Machiavellian power, of course. An insane work ethic. A callous insensitivity to collateral damage, an indifference to the consequences of his actions. A driving ambition and relentless desire to put his mark on the roads and parks and skyline of New York. But beyond that, whether you respect him or despise him, you ought to know that one secret to his success was rather simple: having a clean desk.

Actually, as Robert Caro observed, it wasn't technically a desk. Robert Moses preferred to work off a large table, because it made him more effective and encouraged better workflow. Moses believed in *processing*: Something came in and he dealt with it. Mail, memos, reports—he didn't let any of it sit, let alone pile up. "Since a table has no drawers," Caro wrote of Moses's system, "there was no place to hide papers; there was no escape from a nagging problem or a difficult-to-answer letter except to get rid of it in one way or another."

By keeping his desk and office organized, Moses got stuff done.

But you?

You're drowning in papers. Or digitally, your inbox overflows, your desktop is packed with icons, your phone an endless mosaic of apps and programs. Then you wonder why you're stressed, why you're behind, and why you can't find anything. Precious seconds—piling up into precious minutes and hours—spent shuffling, scrolling, searching, moving. It would be impossible not to be distracted, exhausted by the mess we've decided to wallow in.

Thus the axiom from author Gretchen Rubin: *Outer order, inner calm.*

If we want to think well and work well, it doesn't start with the mind. It starts with walking around and cleaning up.

"I tell my students," Toni Morrison explained, "one of the most important things they need to know is when they are their best, creatively. They need to ask themselves, What does the ideal room look like? Is there music? Is there silence? Is there chaos outside or is there serenity outside? What do I need in order to release my imagination?"

For very few of us—no matter the profession—"When are you at your best?" is answered with "When I am drowning in paperwork, dirty dishes, half-empty water bottles, and floors that haven't been swept." The session in the weight room goes better when the weights are stacked and the dumbbells are in the right place. The craftsman is safer when the workshop is tidy. The team plays better when the locker room is kept up. The meetings run tighter when the conference room is fresh and sparse. The general ensures troop discipline by keeping their own quarters spartan and spotless.

The space where great work is done is holy. We must respect it.

Because a person comfortable with a messy workspace will become comfortable with sloppy work. A person who doesn't eliminate noise will miss the messages from the muses. A person who puts up with needless friction will eventually be worn down.

Of course, this is less about spit and polish than it is about orderliness or *kosmiotes*, as the Stoics called it. Chefs speak of *mise en place*—prepping and organizing everything you need before setting down and getting down to work. Nothing spilling out onto anything else. Nothing random. Nothing getting in the way, nothing slowing anything or anyone down.

Imagine what you could get done if you had the discipline to proactively put everything in order first. If you committed to orderliness and enforced it on yourself. Don't think of that as another obligation, another thing to worry about. Because in practice, it will free you.

Once the systems are in place, once the order is established, then and only then are we able to truly let loose to turn ourselves over to the whims and furies of creativity, to pushing ourselves physically, to audacious invention or investment.

As the novelist Gustave Flaubert commands:

> Be regular and orderly in your life, so that you may be violent and original in your work.

Clean up your desk. Make your bed. Get your things in order. Now get after it.

Just Show Up

The brilliance of Thomas Edison was not in his mind. It was something much more ordinary, and often, much less respected.

"I've got no imagination," he once said. "I never dream. I've created nothing."

If you're someone who doesn't like Edison, you might think that this is Edison admitting to stealing his inventions from other, more brilliant inventors like Nikola Tesla.

Not quite, but he did readily concede that most of the credit belonged to something other than his brain.

"The 'genius' hangs around his laboratory day and night," Edison said. "If anything happens he's there to catch it; if he wasn't, it might happen just the same, only it would never be his."

What he's talking about is *showing up*. The incredible, under-rated power of clocking in every day, putting your ass in the seat, and the luck this seems to inevitably produce. Edison lived in his laboratory and never missed a day—like Gehrig, even when he was sick, when he was tired, or when visited by tragedy or disaster.

The modern conveniences we can trace to his lab then, owe far more to his body than his brain, to the compounding power of consistency rather than sheer brilliance. It wasn't about inspiration. It was about getting to work.

Show up and try. Get on the treadmill. Pick up the violin. Answer some emails. Script out some scenes. Reach out to some clients. Read some reports. Lift a couple weights. Jog one mile. Cross one thing off the to-do list. Chase down a lead.

It doesn't matter what it is; all aspects of our life benefit from this circumscribed kind of discipline. "Just as long as you do something every day, that is the important thing," Arnold Schwarzenegger said to people trying to stay in shape and productive during the endless blur of the pandemic.

Show up . . .

. . . when you're tired

. . . when you don't have to

. . . even if you have an excuse

. . . even if you're busy

. . . even if you won't get recognized for it

. . . even if it's been kicking your ass lately.

Once something is done, you can build on it. Once you get started, momentum can grow. When you show up, you can get lucky.

Is this still hard? Yes. But the good news is that because it's hard, most people don't do it.

They don't show up. They can't even do one tiny thing a day.

So yes, you're alone, out there on the track in the rain. You're the only one responding on Christmas. But having the lead is, by definition, a little lonely.

This is also why it's quiet in the morning. You have the opportunities all to yourself.

Don't worry about setting any records . . . just report for duty. No excuses. And here's the irony: This is also a way to break records!

Consistency is a superpower. Day-to-day willpower is incredibly rare. Lou Gehrig was a solid position player and a good hitter.* But his success really was rooted in the fact that he didn't miss many days of work. It's quite likely that had he continued at his normal pace and not been stricken with ALS that he would have put up career numbers that surpassed Babe Ruth's.

Gehrig wasn't just able to show up despite injuries and fatigue. He also had to push through ennui, doubt, and just plain *not feeling it.* He had slumps, like we all do, but he also understood what they meant. As a minor leaguer, he had struggled at the plate and thought about quitting. The Yankees's owner sent

---

*Much of this is also true about Cal Ripken Jr., who broke Gehrig's consecutive games played streak fifty-six years later.

down a scout to walk Gehrig through the very basic math of a batting average. A good hitter hits .300, and hitting .350 is terrific. Hitting .400 is almost unheard of. What does that translate to? *Missing on six tries out of ten.*

A hitter can also go days, weeks, without touching the ball! That's what the scout told him:

> The most important thing a young ball player can learn is that he can't be good every day.

You don't have to always be amazing. You *do* always have to show up. What matters is sticking around for the next at bat.

The ability to do that, coupled with the ability to endure what John Steinbeck called "dawdly days" while writing *East of Eden*—those days when everything seems out of whack, when you're just not feeling it, when the distractions won't stop—is the first step to greatness.

Literally.

You cannot be great without the self-discipline to do that.

One thing a day adds up. Each day adds up.

But the numbers are only interesting if they accumulate in large quantities.

Sweat the Small Stuff

~

Even though they were some of the best recruits in the nation, even though they'd been doing this nearly every day of their lives, Coach John Wooden started his very first team meeting at the beginning of each UCLA season with a simple exercise.

"Men," he said, "this is how you put your shoes and socks on."

This, certainly, was not what they expected. Not the kind of instruction they thought they'd get from one of the winningest coaches in the history of sports. But it was actually exactly what they needed, and as they eventually came to understand, the real secret to success both on the court and in life.

In basketball—a game played on a hard floor—an athlete's footwear is incredibly important. An improperly worn shoe can lead to a blister, which can lead to an infection, to favoring a foot, to going up for a rebound wrong, to a broken ankle or a blown-out knee.

"It took just a few minutes," Wooden explained, "but I did show my players how I wanted them to do it. Hold up the sock, work it around the little toe area and the heel area so that there are no wrinkles. Smooth it out good. Then hold the sock up while you put the shoe on. And the shoe must be spread apart—not just pulled on the top laces. You tighten it up snugly by each eyelet. Then you tie it. And then you double-tie it so it won't come undone—because I don't want shoes coming untied during practice, or during the game."

Of course, we all think we're past this.

We have something more important to think about. We want something more exciting to do. Less basic, less fundamental.

We want to *really* challenge ourselves, not waste time running through some checklist, stretching before a workout, reading the instructions instead of diving in.

But that's the point: We're fit to tackle the big problems only if we do the little things right first. No strategy will succeed—however brilliant—if it ignores *logistics.*

"The devil is in the details," the great admiral Hyman Rickover used to say, "but so is salvation."

And as the reckless and irresponsible Zelda Fitzgerald said with only some self-awareness, the opposite is also true. "It is the loose-ends," she lamented, "with which men hang themselves."

By focusing on form, by sweating the small stuff, we make ourselves stronger—stronger, in fact, than if we'd just rushed in and thrown ourselves at supposedly harder problems. By ignoring the little things, we make ourselves vulnerable.

Is anything made better by inattention? the philosopher Epictetus would ask. *Of course not!* Whether you're a carpenter or an athlete, an investor or an infantry officer, greatness is in the details. Details require self-discipline. Even if nobody else notices . . . or cares.

Dating back perhaps to time immemorial is the poem and proverb about a horse. "For want of a nail, the shoe was lost," it begins. And then because of the shoe, the horse was lost and because of the horse, the rider and because of the rider, the message and because of the message the battle and because of the battle, the kingdom. *For want of a nail, the kingdom was lost.*

Because of a blister, the game was lost.

Because the little things were ignored, because discipline lapsed, everything was lost.

Save yourself. Save the world. Get the little things right.

Hustle, Hustle, Hustle

~

It is the most maddening thing, and yet it fills the letters and dispatches in almost every conflict that has ever been waged. Out of fear, out of laziness, out of poor management, a general just won't get their troops moving. It's what they trained for their whole lives—to fight—and when the moment comes, they're slow.

In the American Civil War, General George McClellan, for instance, seemed utterly incapable of getting to the fight quickly, to the complete exasperation of everyone who worked with him. Joking to his wife after visiting the general in the field, Lincoln poked fun at his parked commander. "We are about to be photographed [if] we can sit still long enough," he said. "I feel General M. should have no problem." Only after repeated prods from Lincoln—by "sharp sticks," one of his secretaries said—did McClellan finally begin to move against Lee in 1862, taking nine days to cross the Potomac. "He's got the *slows*," Lincoln said in frustration.

McClellan was a brilliant soldier. But groaning under the

weight of his baggage train, his conservatism, his entitlements, his paranoia, and his precaution, he was constitutionally unable to do things quickly, to act urgently, to care about the people waiting on him. Worse, when he did move against the enemy, it was only half-heartedly and he often stopped short, as he did after Antietam, when he had landed a serious blow on Lee's army but declined to follow it up.

He had all the resources, all the talent, all the manpower.

His heart just wasn't in it.*

He was courageous under fire, sure, but not courageous enough to start or finish a battle he knew he might lose. He wasn't disciplined enough to push himself.

In the end, war—as well as life—is about getting up and going. About diving in, even it's scary or hard or uncertain.

Military commanders speak of the value of *celerity,* moving with swiftness and aggressiveness. On the wall in the kitchen at Per Se, one of the best restaurants in the world, is the motto: *A sense of urgency.*

The other, more practical word for this is *hustle.* Whether in business or in sports or combat, all the greats have it. Those who don't? We lament *what could have been.*

Inevitably, the person who *chooses* when to try and when not to is liable to choose incorrectly and betray their team, as Manny

---

* Some speculate that McClellan wanted both sides to exhaust themselves, and with a negotiated peace, preserve the Union with slavery intact.

Machado did in a National League Championship series game in 2018. "I'm not the type of player that's going to be 'Johnny Hustle,'" Machado told reporters after being thrown out half-jogging after hitting a ball deep in the hole to shortstop, "and run down the line and slide to first base. That's just not my personality, that's not my cup of tea, that's not who I am."

Imagine what Lou Gehrig would have thought about that? "Always run them out. You never can tell," was the commandment of the Yankees clubhouse. A great player shouldn't even need to be reminded of this—it should be in their blood. "There's no excuse for a player not hustling," Gehrig would say. "I believe every player owes it to himself, his club, and to the public to hustle every minute he is on the ball field."

If you're not a person who hustles, who are you? Where does that leave the people counting on you?

Although Machado signed a huge contract the next year in free agency, it wasn't with the Yankees, who were his first choice. The team's owner explained why: Not hustling "ain't going to sell where we play baseball."

It's easy to judge and to criticize as a fan, but that's not the only role that sports (or the study of warfare) has to play in our lives. This should serve as a mirror.

There is a bit of McClellan in all of us. A bit of Machado in all of us. We get tired. We get scared. We know it's going to be hard. We get entitled and vain. We don't see the point. We don't want to look foolish.

We have to push through that.

You may lose battles, Napoleon said, *but never lose a minute to sloth.*

Few of us hustle as much as we could. Are you someone whom colleagues and clients can count on to be there when they need you? Or will they have to prod? Will they have to beg? Will they have to repeat, again and again, *the urgency* of the situation?

And what will it say about you if they do?

So let's push ourselves to be better, to get after it. Hustle because we care. Because we care about the game. Because we care about the cause.

We hustle because you never know—when it will make a difference, when someone might be watching, when it might be our last try, when "the slows" might cost us everything.

We should always run them out. Run, period.

Because it's who we are.

Slow Down . . . to Go Faster

Octavian was just eighteen years old when he was named Julius Caesar's heir. At nineteen, at the Forum to Rome's elite, where motioning to his adoptive father's statue, he swore he would match him accomplishment for accomplishment. This was a young man going places—*going places in a hurry*, as the expression goes. And yet, he did not become the famed *Augustus,* or "the venerable," by moving quickly.

Not like you'd think anyway. His rise from pretender to the throne was, in fact, a remarkably methodical and patient one, advised as he was by two great Stoic teachers, Athenodorus and Arius Didymus. He spent ten years sharing power with Mark Antony. He spent nearly five years as *Princeps senatus* (leader of the Senate). Then finally, in 27 BC, he declared himself Augustus Caesar.

A dazzling rise that, unlike most of his predecessors and successors, actually stuck. Because it was in accordance with his favorite saying, *festina lente*. That is, to make haste *slowly*.

As we learn from the historian Suetonius, "He thought nothing less becoming in a well-trained leader than haste and rash-ness," Suetonius wrote. "And, accordingly, favorite sayings of his were: 'More haste, less speed'; 'Better a safe commander than a bold'; and 'That is done quickly enough which is done well enough.'"

Yes, it's important to hustle. We can't tarry or delay or de-velop a case of the slows. Yes, we must run with swiftness. At the same time, our path also requires disciplined pacing. The per-son who rushes, the person who puts efficiency over efficacy, who ignores the "small stuff" is, in the end, not very efficient.

When Octavian took over Rome, it was a city of bricks. He was proud, he said, to leave it a grand empire of marble. It took time, it took getting a lot of small things right, but it was worth it.

It's easy to go fast. It is not always *best.*

They like to say in the military that slow is smooth and smooth is fast.

Do it right and it goes quickly. Try to go too quickly and it won't go right.

How do you balance hustle with *festina lente*?

Perhaps it's best embodied in a different Civil War general, General George Thomas. Thomas was hardly known for his speed. His nickname, in fact, was "Old Slow Trot," which he had earned for the discipline he enforced as a cavalry com-mander. But it really wasn't that he was slow; he was deliberate. He wouldn't be knocked off his block, nor would he be deterred from his cause. That's how he earned his other nickname, the

"Rock of Chickamauga," for standing fast against a massive enemy attack that would have easily broken a fair-weather general like George McClellan. Thomas found himself at odds with Grant for not moving fast enough against General Hood's army at Nashville, taking such an exasperatingly long time to get moving on Grant's order to "attack at once" that Grant moved to personally relieve him.

Yet, this was unfair to Thomas, and precisely why it is too simple to say that one must hustle always. Grant thought that Thomas wasn't hurrying, that he was dragging his feet. In fact, he was fully committed, moving slowly only because he was first getting everything right. Having prepared properly, supplied adequately, trained effectively, he waited for the right moment, and *then* attacked with all deliberate speed. Thomas annihilated his enemy in the Battle of Nashville, one of the great victories of the war, in December 1864.

Old Slow Trot was a rock. One that, once it got rolling, nothing could block.*

That's *festina lente*.

Energy plus moderation. Measured exertion. Eagerness, with control.

"Slowly," the poet Juan Ramón Jiménez would say, "you do

---

* Thomas died of a stroke in 1870 in the middle of writing a letter defending himself against an accusation that he had ever given anything less than his best in the war.

everything correctly." That's true with leadership as well as lifting weights, running as well as writing. Hustle isn't always about hurrying. It is about getting things done, *properly*. It's okay to move slowly . . . provided that you never stop. Do we not understand that in the story of the tortoise and the hare, that it was actually the turtle who hustled? The hare was Manny Machado or George McClellan. Brilliant, fast even in bursts, but not consistently so.

"Doing things badly," Jiménez would say to critics or editors or even impatient readers, "does not give you the right to demand haste from the person who does them well."

And so we must have this attitude not only toward other people—our boss, the audience, the suppliers—who want us to rush, but also the part of ourselves that so loves *doing,* that we just wanted to get started before we were ready. The part of us that loves the fight, that loves the action, that wants to get straight to the work.

Of course, having this impulse is better than not having it, but if it is not properly managed, it will turn from an asset to a liability.

Practice . . . Then Practice More

~

It is said that the master swordsman Nakayama Hakudo would practice drawing his sword some two thousand times a day. At the Hayashizaki temple, in one marathon of endurance training, he was recorded drawing his sword *ten thousand times* in a single twenty-four-hour period.

We can imagine the sheer speed required to do this . . . and also the deliberateness to do so many reps in so little time. But why would he do such a thing at all?

Because, as Octavian's teacher Arius Didymus said, "Practice over a long time turns into second nature."

We don't rise to the occasion, we fall to the level of our training.

The samurai Musashi was once challenged by a warrior named Miyake Gunbei, a man who thought himself one of the best in the world. On his third attack, frustrated by his lack of success, Gunbei charged at Musashi in an aggressive lunge. Musashi, having prepared for this exact scenario countless times, replied, "That is not what you should do," then parried the blow with one sword and watched as the man gashed his own cheek against Musashi's other sword.

How had he known?

Practice.

Cho tan seki ren was Musashi's phrase. *Training from morning to night.*

Oh, you've done that? Okay. Do it some more.

And after that?

More. More. More.

"A thousand days of training to develop," Musashi would write, "ten thousand days of training to polish." For a samurai, there was no such thing as *pretty good.* If a pretty good swordsman met a better fighter . . . he would die. It's like the basketball Hall of Famer Bill Bradley's observation: When you are not practicing, refining, working—somewhere, someone else is . . . and when you meet them, they will beat you.

Or kill you.

Gunbei was lucky enough to learn this lesson and live to tell about it. In fact, after Musashi treated the man's wound, Gunbei accepted that he was outmatched and became Musashi's student, training and practicing under him until he was no longer prone to the mistakes that come from such rashness.

Look, this is not a drill. There is no greatness without practice.

Lots of practice.

Repetitive practice.

Exhausting, bone-crunching, soul-crushing practice.

And yet what emerges from this practice is the opposite of those three feelings.

Energy.

Strength.

Confidence.

You deserve that. Yes, your body will burn, but that's the evidence. From that burning comes real heat, heat you can apply to your craft, to your work, to your life.

The cellist Pablo Casals practiced continually late into his life, even long after he was widely considered a master, because he believed he was still making progress. In fact, we might say that progress and practice are synonyms. You can't have the former without the latter. And the latter is worthless without the former.

Drawing the sword from the scabbard. Thrusting. Blocking. To build up your stamina for those skills, you lift weights, you do conditioning. To put it all together, you spar. It's the same with music. You can jam with other talented musicians, you can put all those sessions together to learn new songs. But before all that, as Casals did, you can simply practice your scales in your bedroom for hours upon hours. What are those scales for you? You better know and you better be doing them.

No matter what you do, practice will make you better. Florence Nightingale wanted young nurses to understand that nursing was an art that required "as hard a preparation as any painter or sculptor's work." Churchill spent many evenings practicing his "impromptu" performances.

Only you know what it will look like to train in your art like a samurai, an Olympic athlete, a master in pursuit of excellence. Only you will know what you need to practice from morning until night, what to repeat ten thousand times.

It won't be easy, but in that burden is also freedom and confidence.

The pleasure of the flow state. The rhythm of second nature.

The quiet calmness of knowing that, from the practice, you'll know exactly what to do when it counts . . . the pride and the dependability of doing it too.

Just Work

~

It is said that no profile of the writer Joyce Carol Oates can begin without mentioning how many books she's published. But this has been true since at least the seventies, and she has not stopped publishing.

Her first book, *With Shuddering Fall*, was released in 1964. By the 1980s, she was up to nineteen books. By the '90s, twenty-seven. In the first decade of the 2000s, she released ten more books. In the following decade, eleven more. In that time, she also published nearly a dozen more novels under pseudonyms, forty-five short story collections, twelve poetry collections, eleven novellas, nine plays, six young adult novels, and four children's books. Even into her eighties, she is still working. How many words must that be in total? Fifteen million? Twenty million?

But that's what the greats do, they don't just show up, they do more than practice, *they do the work.*

Her peers, often more famous and male, attended fancy parties. They had scandalous affairs. They cultivated their literary personas. They despaired over writer's block. They nursed addictions. Joyce Carol Oates worked and taught. Taught and worked.

She *published.*

"I come from a part of the world where people did work rather than just talk about it," she said. "And so if you feel that you just can't write, or you're too tired, or this, that, and the other, just stop thinking about it and go and work."

Which is what Oates has done, nearly every day thus far of her fifty-eight-year career. Grinding down pencils and pens as she wrote first drafts longhand, wearing through typewriters and then laptops as she polished her manuscripts.

In ancient Greece, there was not only a word to describe this kind of ceaseless work ethic—*philoponia*—there were even awards for it. It's this love of toil, of the process that defined someone like Lou Gehrig. It was the reporter Dan Daniel, who asked Gehrig in 1933, whether he had any idea how many games he'd played in a row. Gehrig guessed several hundred. In fact, it was already more than double that. The same is likely true for Oates: If asked how many books she'd written, she'd probably undercount. That isn't how she thinks. She thinks about the work, *el trabajo gustoso,* as one writer put it—the pleasurable work—not what has come out the other side.

"I have always lived a very conventional life of moderation," she explained, "absolutely regular hours, nothing exotic, no need, even, to organize my time. We each have a twenty-four-hour day, which is more than enough time to do what we must do."

Today, we're more apt to talk about work than lose ourselves in it. We like to make a big show of it on social media. We spend a lot of money acquiring the right tools or setting up a fancy office.

Getting down to it? Every day?

That sounds like torture.

Sometimes it *is* torture!

There are days when the words don't come easy, there are days when the vulnerability makes you ache. There are the days when, especially in Oates's case since she writes longhand, that your fingers ache and your eyes blur. But she wouldn't have it any other way.

If you do it right, it's also torture *not* to do it. The sled dog gets anxious if it doesn't get to wear its harness. The horse wants to go out and trot. The bee dies if cut off from the hive. When you find what you're meant to do, *you do it.*

The dancer Martha Graham would tell a story about her vaudeville days, when she was followed by a bird act. When the music went on, the white cockatoos, trained by years of reinforcement and ritual, would become almost hysterical with excitement, clawing and beating at the cage until it was time for them to go onstage and perform. *"Birds, damnit, birds!,"* she would yell at students who didn't give their full commitment. The birds can't want it more than you can.

Some ask, What is the reward for all this labor? They are incorrect if they think it's awards and fame and weeks on the bestseller list. Others want a guarantee: If I put in my ten thousand hours, then I'll get the job? Then I'll be able to go pro? Then I'll be rich? No, that's not how this goes.

Always and forever, the reward is the work. It is a joy itself. It is torture and also heaven—sweaty, wonderful salvation.

And that's how you manage to do prodigious amounts of it—not grudgingly, but lovingly.*

"I'm not conscious of working, especially hard, or of 'working' at all," Oates said. "Writing and teaching have always been, for me, so richly rewarding that I don't think of them as work in the usual sense of the word."

We don't get anywhere in this life without work. But we can get somewhere magical when we do the kind of work that doesn't even feel like work. When we follow the excitement that gets us into the harness, that gets us out in the fields, when we follow the urge to get moving and get at it.

Decide who you want to be, the Stoics command us, *and then do that work.*

Will we be recognized for it?

Maybe, but that will be extra.

---

* Bruce Springsteen, one of the hardest-working musicians in the business, still notes that it's called "playing" for a reason.

Dress for Success

⌒

Angela Merkel grew up in East Germany before the fall of communism. Basic luxuries were not available. Informers made it clear that it was best to not to stand out for anything, especially for how one dressed.

In 1990, she entered politics, emerging from behind the Berlin Wall and the insular world of academia, where she had worked for many years as a quantum chemist. Suddenly, all sorts of attention was paid to how she looked, much to Merkel's surprise. When one political advisor attempted to encourage her to improve her style, Merkel was mortified.

In Eastern Bloc countries, one simply did not do such things. Yet a politician *must* do such things. Especially, as the double standard dictates, a female politician.

A reporter once inquired why Merkel was so often seen in the same pantsuit—don't you have anything else? "I am a civil servant," Merkel replied, "not a model."

Yet she is also savvy enough to refer to politics as a "show." And she has decided to put on an unusual one.

She dresses plainly. She ignores trendy or expensive designers. She favors comfortable shoes. She kept her boxy haircut. She showed up at the office or on television most days, just as God made her—no makeup, ready to work. It's a simple look . . . but always professional. Always proper.

There's a joke that both critics and fans of Merkel like to tell:

What does Merkel do with her old clothes?
She wears them.

People noticed her appearance . . . so she used it to make a statement about modesty and authenticity. Some people get caught up in the game, some people think it is beneath them. Merkel just figured out how to play it in her own sober and authentic way.

The Stoics rejected the idea—popularized by the Cynics—that the philosopher had to reject the standards and fashions of society. While the Cynics went around in rags, the Stoics dressed like normal people. It was whether what was on the *inside* was different that mattered.

Still, they abstained from needless luxury or silly fads. Gaius Musonius Rufus said that "one ought to use clothing and shoes in exactly the same way as armor, that is for the protection of the body and not for display. Therefore just as the most powerful weapons and those best calculated to protect the bearer are the best, and not those which attract the eye by their sheen, so likewise the garment or shoe which is most useful for the body is best, and not one which causes the foolish to turn and stare."

A leader must sweat the small stuff but also must know what stuff matters only to small people. How we dress and style ourselves is one of those tricky edge cases that make "temperance" difficult to pinpoint. A person who is sloppy and slovenly can hardly be said to be particularly self-disciplined. But on the other hand, those who value the superficial—sharp creases, brand names, or the fanciest new styles—over the substantive are equally off track.

Maybe that's why Steve Jobs picked out one comfortable sweater and a brand of jeans and stuck with them all his life. They weren't cheap. They fit well. They worked in every situation. They were timelessly in style . . . and then he never thought about them again.

General Zachary Taylor hated wearing a uniform and disliked displaying his rank or honors—which were considerable. Yet when he met with Commodore David Conner on the Rio Grande during the Mexican-American War, Taylor dressed up to make his guest more comfortable, as full dress was more expected for naval officers. Meanwhile, Commodore Conner, in a gesture of respect to his peer's humble style, came in civilian dress! All of which is to say that every situation, every person may require a different approach.

Most of the time we're not "in the field." Sometimes we're

at a job interview, or appearing on camera, or meeting someone important. Just because we don't put much stock in superficial things doesn't mean that other people's impressions don't matter—especially if we are trying to accomplish something or convince someone of something. Presentation counts . . . and so do other people's feelings. It's not *everything*, but you ignore it at your peril.

And there can be something about cleaning up—a nice shave, freshly ironed garments—that puts us in the right headspace, too, just as cleaning up our desk can work wonders for our productivity and focus. This was why Joe McCarthy, the manager of Gehrig's Yankees, banned shaving in the locker room. Not because he wanted unshaven athletes; on the contrary, he demanded they show up shaven and ready to get to work. Nobody does their best in their bathrobe . . . which is why we ought to take a shower and get ready in the morning, even if we're not going to leave the house. Shine your shoes . . . until *you* are the one glowing.

While the world is unpredictable, one thing we do control is how we take care of ourselves. Making our bed, tucking in our shirt, running a comb through our hair, these are little things we can always do, practices that instill order and cleanliness in a messy situation.

POWs and Holocaust survivors have spoken about how they tried to find ways to keep clean and maintain little parts of their appearance, even amid the filth and horror of their circumstances. No one would accuse them of vanity for doing this; instead we understand it as a courageous assertion of the dignity their captors desired to steal from them.

Sweat the small stuff . . . but don't be superficial.

Welcome to temperance. It's a balance of opposites, by definition.

Sometimes we have to be a bit of Commodore Conner, and sometimes we have to be General Taylor. We have to pull off what Angela Merkel has figured out: how to play the game of appearances without being distracted or consumed by *appearance*.

We dress well . . . but not too well.

We take care to take care of ourselves . . . but never at the neglect of the people or things in our care.

We take our appearance seriously . . . without taking ourselves seriously. As they say in fashion circles, we wear the suit, the suit doesn't wear us.

We look sharp to stay sharp, to be sharp . . . because we are sharp.

Seek Discomfort

~

Seneca was a rich man. He inherited estates from his father. He invested well across the Roman empire. He accumulated even greater wealth in the emperor's service.

Yet every so often, for a few days, he would eat only the scantest fare and wear his coarsest clothing. He would actively seek out discomfort, mimicking abject poverty and harsher life conditions. He slept on the ground and deprived himself of everything but bread and water.

Now, you might think that this is just a precious, even condescending hobby for privileged people, like ice baths or camping. But it was a lot more than that. First off, Seneca took pains to make sure the struggle was serious. "The pallet must be a real one," he wrote to a friend advising him to try this voluntary discomfort, "and the same applies to your smock, and your bread must be hard and grimy. Endure all this for three or four days at a time, sometimes more, so it is a genuine trial and not an amusement."

The point was not bragging rights or moral purity. Seneca

knew that the vast majority of his fellow citizens lived quietly and without complaint in exactly the circumstances he was voluntarily experiencing. In fact, this was the point: He wanted to make it clear to himself that that was perfectly possible and normal to endure. By getting up close and personal with what so many of his wealthy friends dreaded, what made them risk averse and anxious, Seneca could say to himself:

Is this what you feared?

More than once, this practice came in handy for Seneca—indeed, eventually it saved his life. As Nero went insane, Seneca made his move to leave, casually offering the entirety of his fortune for his freedom. Nero was shocked—who could give it all up? Who could value honor more than money? Incensed, Nero would later attempt to poison Seneca at his country retreat, but was unsuccessful, we're told, because the man's meager diet of berries and water made it impossible.

But most of us spend our lives building up walls between us and anything unpleasant . . . not understanding how dependent this makes us. The whole point of success, we feel, is to never have to struggle, to have not only what we need but everything we want on demand: hot water. Nice clothes. Food—of the finest ingredients, cooked by the best restaurants . . . delivered to our door in minutes—at the slightest pang of hunger.

This is perfectly fine to enjoy in moderation. Why shouldn't life generally be comfortable? Still, we must understand that the modern world is conspiring against us, working to degrade our ability to endure even the slightest difficulty. It spoils us . . . and sets us up for failure or slavery.

We take the easy way, because it's there. Who would possibly choose to be cold? What's the point of being hot if you can turn on the AC? Why would you needlessly carry heavy things you can get someone to pick up for you? Who walks when they could drive?

A person who understands the value of discipline. A person who is comfortable being uncomfortable.

Go run a marathon.

Sleep on the ground.

Lift something heavy.

Do the manual labor yourself.

Jump in the cold lake.

Success breeds softness. It also breeds fear: We become addicted to our creature comforts. And then we become afraid of losing them. Seneca was no Cato day to day, but he knew from his practice, that he *could* be if he had to.

By seeking out discomfort, we toughen ourselves up. If we're not going to live an utterly Spartan existence day to day then we better at least practice toughness regularly enough that we're not afraid of it. It was his early days as a simple law student that set Gandhi up for his later challenges. He got used to getting by on little. Being hungry or cold. Later, when they threw him in jail, like Rubin Carter, he was ready. There was nothing they could take from him that he had not practiced going without.

All self-discipline begins with the body, but it doesn't just magically happen. It was a skill Socrates cultivated, a muscle he built, through the challenges he sought out, just as Buddha spent countless nights sleeping outdoors and wearing rough robes. This treatment is how you a *temper* a sword, exposing it, for brief instances, to heat and cold, to environments that attack the steel and harden it. And so the best of us become the best by undergoing the same challenges, by forcing our bodies to change and adapt.

The fact of the matter is that someday, life will have serious discomfort in store for us.

Are we going to dread that? Or just be ready?

We train ourselves in self-denial as a form of self-preservation. "Take the cold bath bravely," W. E. B. Du Bois wrote to his daughter. "Make yourself do unpleasant things so as to gain the upper hand of your soul."

The person who has the upper hand of their soul, the person who can go without, the person who does not fear change or discomfort or a reversal of fortune? This person is harder to kill and harder to defeat. They are also happier, more well-balanced, and in better shape.

We must practice temperance now, in times of plenty, because none of us know what the future holds—only that plenty never lasts.

Manage the Load

~

I t cost Gregg Popovich $250,000, but it got him two more division titles and his fifth championship. It also changed the NBA and all of sports.

In 2012, the San Antonio Spurs were coming off a six-game road trip. It was their fourth game in five nights, just twenty-four hours after their victory over the Orlando Magic and seventy-two hours after a double overtime victory over the Raptors, 1,700 miles away in Toronto. It was a compressed sixty-six-game schedule with more back-to-back games than ever before. More than that, in the previous season, two of Popovich's stars, Manu Ginóbili and Tony Parker, had gone straight from the playoffs to the Olympics, where they started for their respective national teams. Tim Duncan, perhaps the best power forward to ever play, was in his sixteenth year in the league. Collectively, they had upward of three thousand professional games among them, and consistently went deep into the playoffs, as part of the Spurs dynasty, which was built around workhorse role playing and sustained excellence.

Popovich's decision to deliberately rest four of his best players during a nationally televised game was shockingly controversial. The team wanted them to play.* The fans were pissed and wanted refunds. The TV announcers were livid, and so were the channels that had paid for the broadcast rights. Other coaches complained, and athletes condemned him. The league's punishment was swift and costly.

But Popovich had the discipline to play a longer game—to strategically rest his athletes so they would have enough gas to make a run deep into the playoffs, and so they could have longer careers and continue to play at an elite level.

The simple name for it: *load management.*

"We've done this before in hopes of making a wiser decision, rather than a popular decision," he told a reporter of what would become a ubiquitous coaching practice. "It's pretty logical."

Logical, yes. Burnout and injuries are way more expensive than time off.

Was it popular? No. And definitely not easy.

When we are committed, when we are driven, when we want to win, self-discipline most often takes the form of getting up earlier and getting more work done. But sometimes, the harder choice, the greater exercise in restraint, is to rest. It's to manage the load instead of throw it on your shoulders (or knees) without

---

*As it happens, the team plane ran into issues and so the athletes were sent home on a Southwest flight.

thinking. Although they come from very different places, the desire to skip a workout and the impulse to work out too much end up in the same place. It's a short-term bargain with long-term consequences, just as the cost of the pleasure of the candy bar or the drug is paid for down the line . . . with interest.

And if that's unaffordable for athletes and their relatively brief careers—think about how much more pronounced this is for the rest of us. We're in this career, we're going to be on this grind for decades. We're in this for *life*.

You think you're getting ahead by taking on a bit more, by pushing a little further. You think it's impressive to push through the little warning signs of pain. No, no, you're missing the point. John Steinbeck referred to this as the "indiscipline of over-work," reminding himself that it was "the falsest of economies."

The proof? Teams that peaked too early. Career-ending injuries. Books that were clearly rushed. Bad decisions made under pressure. Days missed due to preventable illness. Burnout.

Or worse.

Nobody worked harder for America than James Forrestal. He left a career on Wall Street, twice. First to become a fighter pilot in World War I and then in 1940 to be assistant secretary of the Navy. It cost him literally hundreds of thousands of dollars in lost salary, but he did it and revolutionized the Navy in the process, essentially winning World War II as a result. There would have been no success for Eisenhower, nor MacArthur, were it not for the tireless efforts of James Forrestal.

After the war, he became America's first Secretary of Defense, where he was tasked with unifying the armed forces into a single department. It was a job of endless responsibilities and enormous egos, constituting millions of soldiers, civilians, and miles of ocean. Those who observed him could see the toll the job took on him, on his marriage, on anything resembling a life outside the office. "Why don't you go home?" an aide said to him after finding him working late once again. "Go home?" Forrestal replied. "Home to what?"

Instead, Forrestal kept working, working, working; even as the pounds melted off and his skin sallowed and sagged. He was clearly depressed, clearly unsatisfied, clearly struggling, but he pushed on. His decision-making suffered. He rarely smiled. He felt unappreciated. Even when the role ended, as all political appointments do, he couldn't stop. He ground on.

Soon enough, he ended up in the hospital, where he took his own life by jumping out a hallway window. His last words remain unknown to us, but we can see what he was reading, as he left a page from Sophocles marked up, perhaps as a tragic warning to his fellow work-addicts and all of us who have trouble turning *it* off.

Worn by the waste of time—
Comfortless, nameless, hopeless save
In the dark prospect of the yawning grave....

Yes, our work is important. Yes, we hustle. Yes, our drive is how we became successful, our love of the game is what got us here. But without the ability to rein this in, we will not last. We don't just want to be fast and strong now—we want to be fast and strong for a long time.

We want to *keep* winning. But nothing left unchecked lasts for long. Nobody without the ability to self-govern is qualified to govern—that includes not just prodding yourself forward, but also resting yourself, finding balance, listening to your body when it tells you, "I'm about to break!"

Absolute activity, of whatever kind, Goethe said, ultimately leads to bankruptcy.

Even the great Lou Gehrig knew this. Sure, he had the longest streak in baseball, but on many occasions, if he could feel his performance suffering midgame, he took himself out and called for a pinch hitter. His coaches knew this too—famously "raining out" a game on a cloudless day at the Polo Grounds so that Lou might have a day to recover. And of course, there was the off-season, too, a feature of athletic life that those of us in other professions should consider adopting.

No one is invincible. No one can carry on forever.

Each of us can end up like James Forrestal. Even iron eventually breaks down, or wears out.

Do you want people to look at you in a few years, when you are a husk of your former self, and think about *what could have been*?

If you had stayed healthy, if you had had something left in the tank, if you hadn't wasted all that potential . . .

To last, to be great, you have to understand how to rest. Not just rest, but relax, too, have fun too. (After all, what kind of success is it if you can *never* lay it down?)

The most surefire way to make yourself more fragile, to cut your career short, is to be undisciplined about rest and recovery, to push yourself too hard, too fast, to overtrain and to pursue the false economy of overwork.

Manage the load.

Sleep Is an Act of Character

~

The night before he fought Archie Moore for the title in 1956, Floyd Patterson executed the single-most important part of his training regime.

It wasn't some last-minute conditioning or another review of the fight plan.

He went to sleep.

Not for a few fitful winks but for *eleven and a half hours,* waking up just in time for the morning weigh-in. And before he left for the arena, he took a three-hour nap. And then he napped in his dressing room before he entered the ring, where he knocked out the exhausted champion in the fifth round.

When you're going to go toe-to-toe with one of the best boxers of all time, you better be well rested. When you train as hard as Patterson did, you better make sure you're also giving the body time to recover. Everyone else was nervous. Everyone else was checking and rechecking plans.

But Patterson was asleep. Not because he didn't care about those things, but because he cared the most. While the ability to sleep quickly and rest well might not seem like a matter of discipline, it very much is. In fact, in the armed forces, they refer now to the idea of *sleep discipline.*

It's something you not only have to do, but something you have to enforce in yourself—in terms of both quantity and quality. The higher the stakes, the more driven you are, the more stressful the situation, the more discipline sleep requires.

In the Persian Gulf in the 1990s, future four star admiral James Stavridis had just been given command of a ship for the first time. This occurred at exactly the same time, he noticed, at age thirty-eight, that his natural metabolism and his infinitely youthful ability to just *gut it out*, had begun to decline. You don't have to be the most self-aware person on the planet to see that you make worse decisions when you're tired, that you're less able to work well with others, that you have less command of yourself and your emotions. But it was still a considerable innovation for Stavridis to decide to treat sleep as an equally important part of a functioning warship as its weapons systems.

In response, he began to monitor the sleep cycles of his crew, moderate their watch duties, and encourage naps wherever possible. "Watching our physical health," he would write later, specifically referring to sleep, "is an *act of character* and can enormously help with our ability to perform."

Our moments of peak performance rarely come when we are exhausted, when we are running on fumes, when we are bleary-eyed and dependent on caffeine. And even if they sometimes do, they shouldn't *have* to.

Waking up early to grab those few hours before daylight, before the noise—this is important. But Toni Morrison wouldn't have been able to do that (nor would there have been much point) if she had stayed up late the night before mindlessly watching television. Imagine how much more brilliant Hemingway's mornings could have been, were they not so frequently hungover ones. Certainly Marcus Aurelius's debate with himself about whether to stay under the covers would take on a different meaning had he only just gotten in them a couple hours before.

Meanwhile, we're at home, burned out after a long day. We made dinner. We exercised. We put the kids to bed. We caught up on email. We're so exhausted it feels like all we can do is just veg out on the couch . . . when in fact, we need one final push of discipline: picking ourselves up and walking to the bedroom and passing out.

It will solve so many of your problems. You're tired, so you don't want to work out. You're tired, so you procrastinate. You're tired, so you *need* that coffee, so you pop that pill. You're tired, and you make bad decisions that eat up hours and hours of work that should be spent on the things that matter.

We say "I'm not a morning person," but that is almost certainly because we have been an irresponsible or undisciplined *evening* person. The best way to master the morning is to have mastered it the night before. Just as anyone who has ever sleep-trained an infant learns—sleep begets sleep—so, too, does discipline beget discipline.*

Early to bed. Early to rise.

Under the blankets is no way to fame, Dante said of the morning . . . and yet paradoxically, getting under the blankets consistently, reasonably, without delay is the way to fame. Or at least, to solid performance once one has leapt from bed and out the door.

You want to think clearly tomorrow? You want to handle the small things right? You want to have the energy to hustle?

Go to sleep.

Not just because your health depends on it, but because it is an act of character from which all our other decisions and actions descend.

---

* And the phrase *sleep training* is operative there. It's not something we always do naturally. It takes work, practice, and commitment.

What Can You Endure?

~

In the winter of 1915, Ernest Shackleton's arctic expedition got stuck in the ice. For nearly a year, they drifted aimlessly, the crew powerless to change their condition. Then suddenly the pressure from the ice cracked the hull of their ship and it sank. A 350-mile dash in the lifeboats finally put them on dry land— the uninhabitable Elephant Island—for the first time in eighteen months.

Yet their physical ordeal was not even close to over. In fact, it had only begun.

Unlikely ever to be discovered by passing ships on this remote island, with little to eat and morale dwindling, Shackleton proposed a bold plan: He and a few men would travel more than seven hundred miles to find help.

With only a few weeks' supplies, he and his small crew braved hurricane-strength winds and the open ocean in a twenty-foot boat. Think of his body against the elements, the hunger gnawing at his bones, the aching of his muscles. Arriving in south Georgia in April 1916, he was safe.

But Shackleton knew his mission was only half done. Now, mustering whatever strength and energy he had left, knowing that his men had very little time, he rushed to raise funds and supplies to return to Elephant Island and rescue the men he had left behind.

After four months and multiple desperate attempts, he succeeded—bringing every man on the voyage home alive.

How did he do it? How did he not only survive but emerge unbroken, undaunted, from this experience? His family motto tells us: *Fortitudine vincimus.* By endurance we conquer. Fittingly, this was the name of his ship as well: the *Endurance.*

But imagine those long winter months. Imagine those days at sea. He moved himself through that. He did not quit. He never let his body quit. He ran marathon after marathon after marathon. It wasn't just that he knew what his duties were as captain, he was also strong enough physically, and determined enough temperamentally to fulfill them despite every conceivable obstacle.

Meanwhile, we're tired because we had to put in some overtime at the office. We resent the coach putting us through an extra round of drills. Instead of wanting things to be easy, you should be prepared for them to be hard.

Because they will be!

There is an old German word, *sitzfleisch*, which basically means sitting your butt in the chair and not getting up until the task is complete. Even as it goes numb, even as one by one, the people around you call it a day. Showing up yourself, day after day, until your back aches, your eyes water, and your limbs turn to mush.

Many a great conqueror in the days of horseback were called "Old Iron Ass" for their ability to stay in the saddle.

This is a trait that far too many of us are lacking. We think we can make up for it with brilliance or creativity, but what we really need is commitment. What we need is a willingness to put our body where the problem is, throwing ourselves completely into solving it, to show that we are not for turning, that we will not be deterred.

Almost all great leaders, great athletes, great philosophers, have been tough. They've been able to endure. That's what it takes: sacrifices. Pushing through frustrations. Pushing through criticisms and loneliness. Pushing through pain.

Edison tested six thousand filaments, one by one, in his laboratory, before he found the one that brought us light. Toni Morrison was up early, all those tired mornings, sitting in the chair, watching the sun come up. Shackleton refused to abandon his responsibilities, refused to stop, until he had brought his people home.

It took Franklin Delano Roosevelt seven years of painful physical therapy and exercise to convalesce from polio . . . and each day after, even getting down the hall or stepping up to a podium, was a feat of strength. Think of FDR, struck in the prime of his life with a virus that left him permanently paralyzed from the waist down. Churchill, writing about FDR before the outbreak of the war, would detail the incredible perseverance his seven year recovery required,

> His lower limbs refused to move. Crutches or assistance were needed for the smallest movement from place to place. To ninety nine out of a hundred men such an affliction would have terminated all forms of public service except those of the mind. He refused to accept this sentence.

FDR refused to accept his sentence—he refused to let his body decide who was in charge.

It did not surprise Churchill then, to see the fortitude with which Roosevelt tackled the Great Depression or the "hurly-burly of American politics in a decade when they were exceptionally darkened by all the hideous crimes and corruption of Gangsterdom which followed upon Prohibition." And his energy and enthusiasm in World War II followed still from this too.

Meanwhile, we're ready to call it quits after our first round of submissions are rejected. We consider it a crime against humanity that the profession demands more than forty hours a week. We fold our business after one slow sales period. We declare recovery impossible after the injury. We listen when they say we're not big enough, not pretty enough, not talented enough. We look at the scoreboard and believe that it's hopeless.

Does endurance always conquer?

Of course not, but nobody wins by throwing in the towel. Nobody wins with weakness.

We will taste pain on this journey, that's a fact. We will be given a million opportunities to stop, and a million reasons why that's okay.

But we can't. And it's not.

We keep going.

We put our butt in the chair.

We will not be deterred.

Beyond the Body . . .

~

Those who think that they can live a high spiritual life whose bodies are filled with idleness and luxuries are mistaken.

TOLSTOY

We are mortal beings. This matters not just because it means that each of us will die, but that in order to live, we must do certain things—eat, sleep, move. And of course, the better we do these things, the better care we take of our body, the better shape we'll be in.

It's important to understand that temperance isn't about a life without pleasure. In fact, a major reason we practice self-discipline is so that we might live longer, or at least since that is out of our control, as Lou Gehrig tragically illustrates, that we might live well while we live.

"People pay for what they do," writer James Baldwin wrote,

"and still more, for what they have allowed themselves to become. And they pay for it simply: by the lives they lead."

The fact is, *the body keeps score.*

The decisions we make today and always are being recorded, daily, silently and not so silently, in who we are, what we look like, how we feel.

Are you making good decisions? Are you in control . . . or is your body?

This matters not just physically, but also mentally and spiritually. Temperance in the body affects the mind, and just as much, intemperance and excess physically prevent the mind from working as it should. The neuroscientist Lisa Feldman Barrett has explained it in terms of a *body budget*: Our brain regulates our body, but if we are physically bankrupt, the brain cannot possibly do its job.

If you wonder why people make bad decisions, why they are not resilient, why they are distracted, why they are afraid, why they are caught in the thrall of extreme emotions—if you wonder why *you* do these things—well, it starts with the body.

In addiction circles, they use the acronym HALT—Hungry, Angry, Lonely, Tired—as a helpful warning rubric for the signs and triggers for a relapse. We have to be careful, we have to be in control, or we risk losing it all.

When we speak of temperance and self-discipline, we are

referring to a person who has themselves under control. The body is the first step in that journey.

We treat it rigorously. We restrain it. We dominate it. We treat it like a temple.

Why?

So it may not overrun and override the mind. So it may not deprive the mind.

In that sense, we are constraining ourselves physically . . . to free ourselves mentally and spiritually.

No one who is a slave to their urges or to sloth, no one without strength or a good schedule, can create a great life. Certainly they will be too consumed with themselves to be of much good *for* anyone else. Those who tell themselves they are free to do anything will, inevitably, be chained to something.

Discipline is how we free ourselves. It is the key that unlocks the chains. It is how we save ourselves.

We choose the hard way . . . because in the long run, it's actually the only way.

PART II

THE INNER DOMAIN (THE TEMPERAMENT)

What man is happy? He who has a healthy body, a resource-ful mind, and a docile nature.

THALES

The body is just one vehicle for our self-discipline. History is replete with talented people—athletes, creatives, executives—who had complete command of their physical form but were profoundly a mess everywhere else. It doesn't matter how much discipline we exert over what we eat or when we wake up if we are riven by distraction, at the mercy of biases or bad moods, given over to temptation, impulses, or instinct. This is no way to live—in fact, this intemperance condemns a person to never reach their full potential, with perpetual misery as a possible chaser. True self-control means moderation not just in what we *do*, but also how we think, how we feel, how we comport ourselves in a world of chaos and confusion. If anything, these traits matter more. An observer of Franklin Delano Roosevelt once quipped that the man had a "second-class intellect and a first-class temperament." Given what disease took from Roosevelt's body, the truth of the remark is all the more illustrative: *Temperament is everything.* Our head and our heart combine to form a kind of command system that rules our lives. Millions of years of evolution have combined to give us these gifts. Will we command them as tools? Or will we let them languish, allowing ourselves instead to be jerked around like puppets? You decide.

Ruling Over Yourself . . .

You could say it was in her from the beginning.

Churchill certainly saw it.

Upon meeting the baby who would become the great Queen Elizabeth II, Britain's longest-serving monarch and likely the longest serving in *all* of history, he noted, "She has an air of authority and reflectiveness that's astonishing in an infant."

But of course, the throne then lay some two-and-a-half decades in the future, on the other side of a world war and an abdication crisis. What Churchill sensed that day were the beginnings of the temperament that created an incredible life of self-control, service, and perseverance. A mental and emotional discipline that has rarely been seen, before or since, in the halls of grand palaces, especially in twenty-five-year-olds who have suddenly become empresses or emperors.

We want to think of leaders as bold and brash, charismatic and inspiring. We expect them to be ambitious, we even excuse tragic flaws or disturbing vices, as long as they're winning or entertaining us. This no doubt makes them compelling, but is it the right recipe for stable, sustainable stewardship? Of a nation, a business, a sports franchise? More important, is that the only way?

Plato had a different ideal in mind, asking for a monarch who was "young, and possessed by nature of a good memory, quick intelligence, courage and nobility of manner; and let that quality . . . [temperance] as the necessary accompaniment of all the parts of virtue attend now also on our monarch's soul, if the rest of his qualities are to be of any value."

Born in 1926, Elizabeth had royal blood but no clear path or even expectation to power. Certainly, few pegged her to fulfill that ancient philosopher's ideal. She was the daughter of the second son of King George V. It was only after the rash decision of her uncle Edward VIII to walk away from the crown to marry a twice-divorced Nazi-sympathizer and then the early death of her father, that Elizabeth's destiny was set.

Whatever Churchill had seen in her as a child, whatever Plato hoped for, she would have to cultivate—making, willing herself into *the* Queen Elizabeth, one of most admired and enduring figures on the planet.

From the day of her coronation, Elizabeth would *reign but not rule*, as the expression goes, holding with perfect grace a unique and terrible job. What does the modern British sovereign do? It's hard to say. It's easier to list all the things they *can't* do. She can't pass laws. She can't choose who leads the government. She can't start wars. She's not even supposed to speak about matters of policy. And yet the irony of this powerlessness is all the power required to wield it: The Queen has been duly informed of every action and problem inside the United Kingdom for sixty-nine years, in the form of daily dispatches and weekly conferences with the prime minister; at the same time, she is not allowed to overtly act on any of this information. She cannot, *in any way whatsoever*, involve herself in the matters of state . . . all of which is done literally in her name!

This is precisely what Elizabeth has managed to do with near superhuman dignity through twelve prime ministers, fourteen US presidents, and seven popes. On her twenty-first birthday in 1947, the future queen would detail her commitment to this idea in a now-famous radio address, telling the people of what was then called the British Empire that "I declare before you all that my whole life whether it be long or short shall be devoted to your service and the service of our great imperial family to which we all belong."

A few years later, she would express her sense of duty and place more explicitly: "I cannot lead you into battle, I do not give you laws or administer justice, but I can do something else, I can give you my heart and my devotion to these old islands and to all the peoples of our brotherhood of nations."

Could she have had any idea how long this service would last? What it would take out of her? What it would demand of her? How much heart and smarts would be required?

Lou Gehrig is a hero for his streak of 2,130 games played for the Yankees. Queen Elizabeth has worked every day for nearly seven decades! For her, every day has been game day, some twenty-five thousand in a row. She's visited more than 126 nations. In 1953, on a single royal tour, she traveled forty thousand miles, many of which were by boat. She shook thirteen thousand hands and received tens of thousands of bows and curtsies. She gave and listened to over four hundred speeches. And this was just one of more than a hundred of these royal tours during her reign. In all, she's traveled more than one million nautical miles by sea, and many times that by air. She's met more than four million people (personally had more than two million over for tea) and given more than one hundred thousand awards. Perhaps most impressive, out of hundreds of thousands of engagements, events, appearances, and meals, which were often preceded by long-distance travel and time zone changes, she has fallen asleep in public only a single time . . . at a lecture about the use of magnets in biology and medicine in 2004.*

It goes without saying that the Queen's regular duties take immense physical discipline. "Are you tired, general?" she once asked a noticeably drooping officer accompanying her on an official visit. "No, ma'am," he replied. "Then take your hands out of your pockets and stand up straight," she told him from her five-foot-four perch. Aides have noted that the Queen is as strong as a yak and can endure long periods of standing, even

---

* The year she turned seventy-eight.

into old age. Harold Macmillan, her third prime minister, once exclaimed that the Queen had the "heart and stomach of a man," which is preposterous because not even Lou Gehrig could have put up with her travel schedule.

But this marveling belies what is beneath those physical feats: the mental and emotional discipline that she quietly draws upon on. For instance, it's been said that the Queen has literally never been seen to sweat. This only makes her marathon appearances more impressive. Her body doesn't cool itself off well, but her poise and equanimity keep this fact from us.

How does she do it? On a visit to the United States during the first Bush administration, an American official would accidentally chance upon the Queen in a moment of quiet preparation for what was to be a very long day. "She was standing stock-still," he noticed. "It was as if she were looking inward, getting set . . . This was how she wound up her batteries. There was no chitchat, but standing absolutely still and waiting, resting in herself."

She has also, through the years, innovated in ways that make the long obligations more palatable—because why white-knuckle things if you don't have to? She spends an average of four seconds meeting each person. She's removed needless courses from dinners. She makes sure that speeches come *after* the meal instead of before, so that she can wrap up and sneak out. To palace media officials, she's known as "One-Take Windsor" because, while she never rushes, she thinks through what she wants to do, and then she gets it right the first time.

As they say, work smarter, not harder.

Discipline isn't just endurance and strength. It's also finding the best, most economical way of doing something. It's the commitment to evolving and improving so that the tasks get more efficient as you go. A true master isn't just dominating their profession, they're also doing it with ease . . . while everyone else is still huffing and puffing. After one tricky social encounter, the Queen was commended for being "very professional." "I should be," she said, not impressed by the compliment, "given how long I've been doing it." Don't worry about the Queen, an aide once reassured a diplomat about a long event, "she's trained for eight hours." Actually, she's a tough enough professional to endure it for *eighty years.*

The Briton with the stiff upper lip, the one who can so preternaturally "Keep Calm and Carry On," has become something of a cliché with the passage of time. And while it's always tricky to apply a stereotype to a diverse population, there's no question that the Queen has personified this ideal, keeping an even keel no matter the circumstances. In 1964, she serenely and calmly endured a violent anti-monarchy riot in Quebec. In 1981, she was riding on horseback when a gunman rushed her and fired six shots; eliciting barely a flinch from the Queen in response. In 1966, a heavy block of cement slammed into the roof of the royal car. "It's a strong car," she said as she shrugged it off. In 1982, a deranged intruder entered the Queen's bedroom, bleeding from breaking a window. Woken from a dead sleep, she could have screamed. She could have run. Instead, she politely entertained the man until she could make an attempt to summon security.

But the greatness of the Queen is more than stoic endurance. The Queen is a lively, savvy woman who has managed to thrive in a position that typically brings out the worst of the people who hold it. While few would refer to her as an intellectual—indeed many sneeringly referred to her as "a countryside woman with limited intelligence"—in fact, her quiet brilliance is itself an illustration of her self-discipline.

Starting at an early age, her father brought her into the business of state, treating her as equal. From her teens, she was advised by Churchill, and tutored twice per week for six years in law by one of England's greatest constitutional experts. The Queen, you can be sure, always knows more than she says. In almost every case, she is more experienced and understands the history of an issue better than the prime minister explaining it during their weekly audience. Yet it is they who inevitably do most of the talking and she the listening. Unlike her son, who not only thinks he's smarter than everyone else but often alienates them by insisting on it, she's fine being underestimated. She's patient enough to know she will eventually be vindicated.

Smart? Discipline is a far rarer commodity at the top than brilliance.

Temperament may be less charismatic, but it *survives*. It *stabilizes*.

Still, she famously reads every dispatch in the Queen's "Red Box," in which the most important ministerial documents are delivered to her. Many are boring. Many are mind-numbingly complex. She reads six newspapers each morning. She does this even though no one forces her to, no one would ever quiz her on the contents. She could instead ask for brief summaries. She could skim. But she doesn't. Even though her opportunities to use this knowledge are constitutionally limited, she does it. Why? Because it is the surest way for her to discharge her duty.

There is really only one avenue to affect change available to the Queen, and in her judicious, restrained way, she uses it: by asking questions. If she's concerned about something or objects to it, she requests more information above and beyond what she finds in the Red Box or the press. Sometimes over and over again until, eventually, the potential issue becomes clear to the relevant policy makers. She doesn't blurt out what she thinks ought to be done, yet in time it becomes clear enough.

"Where she's been brilliant is in her quietness," one press secretary would observe. "In a very noisy world where people constantly want to express themselves or overreact, what the Queen has done has been the opposite." She is not empowered to have political opinions yet she is strong enough to do something most world leaders as well as ordinary people are powerless to do: refrain from expressing opinions about things we don't control.

Elizabeth is, you might say, a lifelong student of human

behavior. Instead of being frustrated by the limitations and obligations of her position, the Queen has found freedom in it, channeling that energy to productive ends. Aides will find some event excruciatingly boring. The Queen, on the other hand, will have found something interesting. "Didn't you realize that chap's father was the son of my father's valet?" she'll be found saying with enthusiasm after a long dinner. "Did you see the man's red socks?" she'll ask after a public event. "Why was there an extra director of music in the gallery?" she'll say after a concert, noticing something that even her security team missed. "What happened to the soldier?" she'll ask of a young man who cut his hand on a bayonet, and his commanding officer, who thought himself too important to be concerned with such things, will have no answer.

A weak mind must be constantly entertained and stimulated. A strong mind can occupy itself and, more important, be still and vigilant in moments that demand it.

Of all that the Queen has endured, one might think that, as a traditionalist in the most traditional of professions, she was at least protected from change. In fact, change has been the largest and most continual challenge of her life. For starters, *most* nations on Earth today *did not exist* when she was born. The world has quite literally remade itself during her reign. Her job has been to both preserve her institution while simultaneously adapting it to a rapidly changing future. She is the last bastion of standards, it has been said, and yet almost every one of those standards has been reevaluated, adjusted, and reimagined over the years—in some cases many times.

"Change has become a constant," she said. "Managing it has become an expanding discipline." Perhaps that is why, as part of this discipline, the Royal household has adopted as a kind of motto a quote from the author Giuseppe Tomasi di Lampedusa: "If things are going to stay the same, then things are going to have to change."

We have to understand: Self-discipline is not keeping things exactly as they are with an iron grip. It's not resistance to any and everything. Nor would much discipline be required in a world that always stayed the same. Temperance is also the ability to adjust, to make good of any situation, to find the opportunity to grow and improve in any situation. And to be able to do this with equanimity and poise, even initiative and joy. Because what other choice do we have?

Perhaps the most interesting and symbolic changes of Elizabeth's reign was her decision in 1993 to tax . . . herself!* If discipline is about holding yourself accountable, there is perhaps no better example than the decision of a monarch to propose that her own government tax her estate and income, over the objection of the prime minister himself.

---

*We can also stipulate that, given the colonial origins of their vast fortune, this tax and their considerable charitable giving are the *least* the Royal Family can do.

But that doesn't mean *everything* is up in the air.

"Better not," is a popular phrase inside the palace. As in, *let's not overstep*. As in, *let's not rush into this*. As in, *let's not fix what isn't broken. Let's take all things, including change, slowly.*

This extends to her considerable wealth and fame. Elizabeth is not an ascetic. She lives in a castle, after all. Fate gave her one, so why not enjoy it? Within bounds, this is perfectly possible for a disciplined person.

While easier than grinding poverty, navigating abundance is its own challenge. To manage it, the Queen has had to live by a code, a sense of duty. "I, like Queen Victoria," she has said, "have always been a believer in that old maxim 'moderation in all things.'" Younger members of her family have struggled with this kind of self-control, rebelled against it, in some disturbing cases abdicated even their basic duties as human beings. The idea that you don't get to do everything you want, that some things are nonnegotiable, that the flip side of privilege is duty, and that power must be complemented by restraint—not everyone gets that. And their shameful behavior reminds us of the consequences.

It's easy to be excited. It's easy to express a preference. It's easy to be a mess too. To give yourself over to whim or to emotion or even to ambition. But to keep yourself in check? To hold yourself to standards? Especially when you could "get away" with less? "Is it not much better to be self-controlled and temperate in all one's actions than to be able to say what one ought to do?" Musonius Rufus would say back in ancient Rome. As an advisor to kings and elites, he understood: Plenty of people are "masters" of their universe while lacking the most important power there is ... power over their own minds, power over their own actions and choices.

Still, it's a hard life. Imagine being so exacting, as the Queen must be, that when a speechwriter hands you a draft of an address that begins "I am very glad to be back in Birmingham," you take the time to cross out the word *very*. Because it's not quite true, nor would it be sincere ... or fair to all the other places she has to (or never will) visit.

An ordinary person could get away with a little rhetorical flourish ... but you aren't a Queen if you're ordinary.

The difficulty of that balance! You are unlike anyone, but you have to be relatable to everyone! You have to be approachable at the same time as being above reproach. Head of state and head of church, modern and timeless ... with everyone watching, ready for the slightest mistake!

Does that mean she allows herself no emotion? That self-discipline means a robotic suppression of feeling? Absolutely not. Although the Queen holds herself to high standards, she is remarkably tolerant of breaches of protocol—the fan who reaches out and grabs her, the diplomat who forgets to bow. She is said to be surprisingly very easy to talk to, very quick to put others at ease. Because this, too, is part of the job. It's hard to be her, but she doesn't make that hard for you.

She has received her share of criticism, too, as all public people must expect to endure. Did she run from this? Complain about it? Quite the opposite. In 1992, a painful and difficult year that included the divorces of three of her children, a tell-all memoir published by one of the divorcées, and a fire at Windsor Castle—her so-called *annus horribilis*—the Queen, still smelling of smoke from the fire, took time to specifically point out that accountability from the press was part of her job. "There can be no doubt," she said, "that criticism is good for people and institutions that are part of public life. No institution—City, Monarchy, whatever—should expect to be free from the scrutiny of those who give it their loyalty and support, not to mention those who don't."

And yet she has also reminded the British press that there is a difference between accountability and cruelty. "Scrutiny can be just as effective," she said, "if it is made with a touch of gentleness, good humor, and understanding."

She has tried to respond with such courtesy even when it was not extended in her direction. In 1957, when the Queen was the subject of a controversial editorial that criticized her for being out of step with the times, for her stilted manner of speaking and dependence on advisors, the Queen did not take offense. In fact, she took no public notice of the criticisms at all—even when the controversy grew so great that its author, Lord Altrincham, was assaulted in the streets of London—but she did privately, and subtly, address the legitimate feedback. Some note that even her accent has slowly shifted, becoming less pronounced and aristocratic over time—a rather impressive, if mostly uncredited feat.

No one lasts very long if they are afraid of change, and few are able to change if they are afraid of feedback or making mistakes.

And so here she is, at the time of this writing, ninety-five years old and still going. She has effectively and tirelessly served as head of state for roughly one-sixth of the Earth's surface. She's done so without personal corruption scandals, without affairs, without major missteps.

If there was anyone who deserves retirement, it's her. Yet she keeps going, getting better at the most difficult job in the world as she goes. In 2013, the monarchs of Netherlands, Belgium, and Qatar would abdicate. A pope would follow suit. For the Queen, this was unthinkable. "Oh, that's something I can't do," she said. "I am going to carry on to the end." And so she has . . .

What about you? Where is your discipline? Your poise and grace under pressure? *You're* tired? *You're* in an impossible situation? Get out of here.

There have been plenty of leaders with more power than Queen Elizabeth.

Few, however, have had more restraint. There have been plenty of gluttons, but few as quietly glorious. It was this self-command, this self-abnegation, that made her a ruler her people could be proud of. It saved her from herself, from the temptations of power, sure, and it also helped to help her outlast not just many tyrants but whole forms of tyranny itself.

We have to understand: Greatness is not just what one does, but also what one refuses to do. It's how one bears the constraints of their world or their profession, it's what we're able to do within limitations—creatively, consciously, calmly.

"Most people have a job and then they go home," the Queen once reflected, "and in this existence the job and the life go on together, because you can't really divide it up."

There is no better definition of the path of temperance. It's an all-consuming, full-time thing.

It's the journey of a lifetime, one that gets more impressive (and rewarding) the longer you stay at it.

Look at Everything Like This

~

George Washington saw a lot go wrong.

He lost his father at age eleven. His was under fire for the first time before he turned twenty-two, when an ambush on a French fort along the Ohio River sparked the French and Indian War. The Revolutionary War, though it ended with a victory, was in reality an almost-ceaseless series of defeats or setbacks, from Long Island to Kips Bay, White Plains to Fort Washington. Throughout the nine-year war, he was in painful financial straits and at constant risk of hearing his beloved Mount Vernon might be burned. And then after, as the US government floundered, he was drawn into the scrum of politics and, ultimately, the presidency, where he was subjected to criticism in the press, difficult subordinates, and the demands of voters.

When Washington was twenty-six years old, he watched a play about the Stoics, where he heard a phrase that he'd turn into his lifelong mantra, repeating it to himself in every stressful and challenging situation, whether it was a setback on the battlefield or the infighting between members of his cabinet.

". . . in the calm light of mild philosophy."

It was in the calm and mild light that Washington approached the news that one of his generals was slandering him behind his back. It was in the calm and mild light that Washington dealt with the saddening realization that he and his wife could not have children. It was in the calm and mild light that Washington approached a mob-like meeting of his officers who threatened mutiny against the new American government, slowly, masterfully, talking them back from treason.

In June 1797 alone, Washington found himself writing this reminder out in three separate letters, trying to stop himself from rushing to judgment or losing control of his emotions and instead looking at the situation with the temperament befitting *the father of a country.*

Because like the rest of us, this was not his natural disposition.

Washington was not exempt, a friend said, from the "tumultuous passions which accompany greatness, and frequently tarnish its luster." In fact, fighting them was the first and the most prolonged battle of the man's life. It was also, the man said in his friend's eulogy, Washington's most impressive victory, "so great the empire he had there acquired, that calmness of manner and of conduct distinguished him through life."

The painter Gilbert Stuart spent many hours with Washington in the 1790s as he worked on a portrait of the general. What he found was a fierce, determined, and intense man. As he studied him, Stuart could feel these thunderous passions but was struck by the way that Washington's "judgment and great self-command" subsumed them. That was why so few had seen his temper. Washington wasn't naturally Stoic; he *made himself this way.* Not permanently but anew every minute, every day, in every situation, as best he could.

You think Washington didn't get frustrated or overwhelmed? Of course he did. Think about what he was subjected to!

Yet according to Thomas Jefferson, who often openly fought with Washington, the man never acted "until every circumstance, every consideration was maturely weighed." He had the initial reactions we all do, but he tried to put every situation up for a kind of review, searching for a better light to explain and understand it.

We know that between every stimulus and its response, every piece of information and our decision, there is space. It is a brief space, to be sure, but one with room enough to insert our philosophy. Will we use it? Use it to think, use it to examine, use it to wait for more information? Or will we give into first impressions, to harmful instincts, and old patterns?

The pause is everything.

The one before . . .

   . . . jumping to conclusions

   . . . prejudging

   . . . assuming the worst

> ... rushing to solve your children's problems for them
> (or put them back to sleep)
> ... forcing a problem into some kind of box
> ... assigning blame
> ... taking offense
> ... turning away in fear.

As we've discussed, there is the higher self and the lower self. This aligns with two types of mental processing we do, which psychologists call thinking *fast,* and thinking *slow.* Fast is often the lower self. Gut instinct is the lower self (like Theodore Roosevelt's hesitation to invite Booker T. Washington to the White House because of the political consequences). Slow is the higher self. Slow is the rational, philosophical, principled self. Really thinking about things, really thinking about who you want to be (understanding upon reflection, as Roosevelt did, that such hesitation needed to be overridden).

We pause. We gather ourselves. We put it up to the light. We ask: *Is this true? Is it actually as upsetting as it feels? As scary or annoying as I first thought?*

Don't let fear or anxiety or prejudice decide. Don't let your temper decide. Let your temperament take over. Or rather, let the temperament you're *striving* to have, that you know your position demands you have, do its work.

A leader can't make decisions on impulse. They must lead from somewhere more rational, more controlled than that. That's not to say they won't ever be tempted, that they won't *have* impulses.

It's that they are disciplined enough not to *act* on them. Not until they've been put up to the test, put under or in front of the light.

Whether we're talking about a post on social media or a costly mistake at work, an obvious lie someone tried to deceive us with, an insubordinate employee, a difficult obstacle, a casual insensitivity, or a complex problem, everything must be met with a measured and mellow eye.

Life is going to throw so much at you, as it did to Washington, to Frankl, to Roosevelt, to every parent and person who ever lived.

The question is: How are you going to look at all this? How in control are you of the light under which you must examine the events of life?

Because the answer determines what you'll be able to do . . . and, more important, who you will be.

Keep the Main Thing
the Main Thing

Booker T. Washington was a busy man. He ran the Tuskegee Institute, which he founded. He traveled constantly, to speak to crowds and meet with donors. He lobbied legislators, gave lectures, led fundraising campaigns, and published five books.

How did he manage it all?

It wasn't just endurance and hustle and energy.

It was also the discipline to say the dreaded word *No*.

"The number of people who stand ready to consume one's time to no purpose," he said, "is almost countless."

Some thought him aloof. Some thought him selfish. They said things behind his back.

He was too busy to notice. He knew that the main thing in life was to keep the main thing *the main thing*. Especially when your main thing is uplifting an entire race of people.

But what is the main thing for the rest of us? That is the *main* question.

If you don't know the answer, how can you possibly know

what to say yes to and no to? How can you know what to show up to? What to wake up early for? What to practice? What to endure? You can't. You're winging it. You're vulnerable to every shiny, exciting thing that comes your way, every "I've got a potential opportunity for you," every "It'll only take a minute," every "Thanks in advance," every "I know you're busy but. . . ."

"Anyone who has not groomed his life in general towards some definite end cannot possibly arrange his individual actions properly," the writer Michel de Montaigne reminded himself. If you don't know where you're sailing, the Stoics said, no wind is favorable.

This means first, the discipline to step away and think: *What am I doing? What are my priorities? What is the most important contribution I make—to my work, to my family, to the world?* Then comes the discipline to ignore just about everything else.

Because Booker T. Washington had a strong sense of purpose—educating a generation of black men and women— he had the clarity and the urgency to reject the things that stood to consume his time in the service of some other purpose. Without that, like so many people, he'd have been eaten alive, his time and power picked apart, one request and distraction at a time.

"I wish I knew how people do good and long sustained work and still keep all kinds of other lines going—social, economic, etc.," John Steinbeck once wrote in the middle of the long grind of writing a novel. *How do they do it?*

They don't!

It is impossible to be committed to anything—professionally or personally—without the discipline to say no to all those other superfluous things.

An interview request. A vibrant social media presence. A glamorous dinner party. An exotic trip. A lucrative side venture. An exciting new trend. No one is saying these things won't be fun, that they don't have potential benefits. It's simply that they also carry with them opportunity costs, they require resources and energy that each person has only so much of.

The secret to success in almost all fields is large, uninterrupted blocks of focused time. And yet, how many people organize their days or lives to make this possible? And then they wonder why they are frazzled, unproductive, overwhelmed, always behind.

Here is the inescapable logic: Everything we say yes to means saying no to something else. No one can be two places at once. No one can give all their focus to more than one thing. But the power of this reality can also work for you: Every no can also be a yes, a yes to what *really* matters. To rebuff one opportunity means to cultivate another.

This is the key not just to professional success but also personal happiness. When someone takes "just a few minutes of your time," they aren't just robbing you (though they admit this when they ask to "pick your brain" and thus your pocket). They're also robbing your family. They're robbing the people who you serve. They are robbing the future. The same goes for when you agree to do unimportant things, or when you commit to too much at one time. Except this time, *you* are the thief.

No one made you hop on the conference call. No one forced you to attend this event or accept that award. There's no law that says you have to reply to every email, return every call, have an opinion on every bit of news.

In tech, they speak of "feature creep"—when a founder or a project manager isn't disciplined enough to protect the core concept of an idea and allows too much to be jammed in it. Trying to please everyone, they end up pleasing no one. To try to do everything is to ensure you'll achieve nothing.

This weaker part of ourselves that cannot say no to requests for our time, that tries to go along with everyone, perhaps deep down wants that same excuse—if we agree to *their* thing, then we don't have to answer for the poor performance of *our* thing when it's time for a full accounting. It allows us to say, "Well, if only I weren't so busy . . ."

The self-disciplined part of us, on the other hand, says, like the Queen's motto, "Better not."

Or maybe we just borrow the quip from E. B. White, who was asked to join some prestigious commission. "I must decline," he said, "for secret reasons." A clerk of Sandra Day O'Connor once said with reverence, "Sandra is the only woman I know who doesn't say sorry. Women would say, 'Sorry. I can't do that.' She would just say, 'No.'"

Say no. Own it. Be polite when you can, but own it.

Because it's your life. And because it is your power. By seizing it, you become powerful. More powerful in fact, than some of the most powerful people in the world who happen to be slaves to their calendars and ambitions and appetites. The conquerors who rule over enormous empires but are slaves to solicitations. The billionaires who fear missing out. The leaders always chasing the shiny new thing. Who cares if you have achieved extraordinary things but are punished for it by having even less freedom day to day?

It feels like you're free because you're *choosing*, but if the answer is always yes, that's not much of a choice.

Perhaps this is what makes an anecdote about General James Mattis from his time as secretary of defense so unusual. Mattis, notoriously private and duty-bound, was not interested in doing the rounds of Sunday-morning talk shows that Washington politicians usually line up for like hogs at the trough. He didn't care about his brand. He didn't care about playing the game. No, he wanted to work. He wanted to actually get things done.

Begged, prodded, bothered, and then criticized by administration officials for not helping them get messages out, he finally called the media office and very calmly reiterated his "No."

"I've killed people for a living," he explained. "If you call me again, I'm going to fucking send you to Afghanistan. Are we clear?"

And that was the end of that.

No one can say yes to their destiny without saying no to what is clearly someone else's. No one can achieve their main thing without the discipline to make it *the main thing*.

Focus, Focus, Focus

~

Ludwig van Beethoven would be in the middle of a conversation and then just disappear. Even if he was talking to a woman he was in love with, or some powerful prince or patron. When an important musical idea came to him, he would lock into it, be consumed by it, almost like he was in a trance. So instant and so deep was his focus.

Are you even listening to me, a friend once asked. Sorry, Beethoven replied, "I was just occupied with such a lovely, deep thought, I couldn't bear to be disturbed."

They called this his *raptus.* His flow state. His place of deep work. The source of his musical greatness. He was being seized by the muses, but also seizing them in return, refusing to let go until he had gotten what he needed.

Now, it might seem a little indulgent, even undisciplined, for an artist to simply check out like this—to be at the whim of their passing thoughts. But it's actually an act of immense self-control and focus. It's easy to stay on the surface. It's easy to be distracted with distractions.

To respect the muses when they visit? To truly focus on your main thing? To ignore everything else and to follow a flit of inspiration or put brainpower toward some intractable problem you can't seem to make progress on? This is the mental challenge we have to steel ourselves for. This is what we have to cultivate the ability to do. To commit. To truly, fully, completely commit.

Because it is extremely rare.

In a world of distraction, focusing is a superpower.

People say they're focused but then . . .

. . . their phone pings

. . . they get distracted

. . . they get tired

. . . they try to multitask

. . . they don't actually have the discipline to truly lock into something.

Keeping the main thing the main thing is not enough. Once the plate is cleared, you must be able to put your whole mind into that main thing. It has to get *all* of you. The Stoics tell us that we must learn how to focus in every moment like a Roman, to seize this thought, this opportunity that is in front of us. We can't waste it. We have to winnow our thoughts, we have to narrow our gaze to what matters and commit to it.

In yogic tradition, this is called *Ekāgratā*—intense focus on a singular point. The ability to put your mind *fully* into or onto something, allowing you to understand both it . . . and yourself in a new way.

Beethoven wasn't just known for drifting off in social conversations, but also for profound, concentrated periods of focus on a single piece of music. A symphony doesn't simply write itself. No flash of inspiration or single moment of *raptus* would be sufficient. It took hours, days, months, *years* of prolonged and exclusive dedication to every facet of the project. There is even some tragic irony in Beethoven's legendary focus. As his hearing declined, it went unnoticed by many of even his closest friends, because they assumed he was simply lost in his work. They believed he *could* hear them had he wanted to. They took for granted that he was just tuning the world out—as he had for so many years—to focus on what he really needed to hear: the muses.

All artists and leaders have to develop this skill. Although Goethe and Beethoven did not get along particularly well, they were both similar in this ability. One biographer describes Goethe as an "expert at ignoring things." Both he and Beethoven combined this with their ability to commit to their art, and to lock into the task or project in front of them, to legendary results.

It's just a fact. The muses never bless the unfocused. And even if they did, how would they notice?

We joke about the absentminded professor, as if they're somehow less together than normal people. It's actually the exact opposite. They are showing us what full commitment looks like in practice. The rest of us are far too concerned with things that don't matter to recognize that true mental discipline comes at a cost—and they are the ones willing to pay it. So they might not be able to find their car keys or they put on mismatching socks? In the end, what will they most likely be remembered for? The occasional social faux pas? Or the transformative work that results from their focused commitment?

Every waking minute, every ounce of brainpower has been marshaled toward the enormous problems they are trying to solve, or to the research they are pioneering, or to the musical revolution they are defining with each measure and movement. That means not just saying no to things but saying *yes* to the critical task in front of you so emphatically, so completely, that you don't even notice that the things you've said no to even exist. Jony Ive, the top designer at Apple would explain that "focus is not this thing you aspire to . . . or something you do on Monday. It's something you do every minute." Steve Jobs, he recounted, would always be asking Ive and other Apple employees about what they were focused on and specifically, "How many things have you said no to?" because to focus on one thing requires *not* focusing on other, less important things.

Epictetus reminds us that when you say, *I'll get serious about this tomorrow* or, *I'll focus on it later,* "what you're really saying is, 'Today I'll be shameless, immature, and base; others will have the power to distress me.'"

No, if it's worth doing, it's worth concentrating on today. It's worth focusing on *now*.

Because like Beethoven, none of us know how many good years we have or how long our faculties will last. We must use them while we can.

Wait for This Sweet Fruit

~

Joyce Carol Oates is one of the most prolific and dedicated writers of her generation, yes.

But would this be admirable if she simply rushed her books out?

Obviously not. Prolific cannot be a euphemism for sloppy.

It's not simply that Oates shows up and writes a lot. There is, on top of this hard, physical labor, serious mental discipline that moderates her drive to create and polish what she ultimately *publishes.*

"I almost never publish immediately," she explained. Each one of her manuscripts, after the completion of the first draft, is placed in a drawer, where it sits, sometimes for a year or more. There, it gestates. Oates thinks about other projects. She explores other ideas. She reads more. Researches more. Lives more. Thinks more.

It's not that these first drafts aren't good. It's that we must always doubt our first burst of excitement and indeed, anything that comes easily. Oates's patience is about acquiring perspective, about giving all the tiny decisions that go into a book enough time to get them right.

It may be that she adds a few pages. It may be that she cuts whole characters or scenes. Most of the time, the changes are very minor. But the precautionary process is essential, as it is with any meaningful act of creation. When Lincoln wrote the Emancipation Proclamation, he not only waited for the right political and military moment to deliver it, but he put it aside multiple times as he was writing, like a painter with their sketches, he said, from time to time adding a line or two, "touching it up here and there, anxiously watching the progress of events."

Was this easy? Waiting for the right moment, whether one is a writer or a politician, is an agonizing thing. But as Aristotle reminds us, "Patience is bitter, but its fruit is sweet."

No matter what it is that we do, we will have to cultivate, beyond hustle and hard work, the discipline of patience. It may well be that this soft skill challenges us more than the hours in the chair or the years of grinding. When your instinct is to *go,* when you really want to *get after it,* waiting . . . well, *the waiting is the hardest part.*

To wait for news.

To wait for the right opportunity.

To wait for things to settle.

To wait for the solution to come to you.

To wait for people to come around.

To wait while you check your assumptions.

To wait and see if you think better of it.

What do we get out of waiting?

Well, the Bible says that through our patience we come to possess nothing less than our souls.

The discipline of patience prevents us . . .

. . . from acting on insufficient information

. . . from picking the wrong option

. . . from going too soon

. . . from forcing it

. . . from rushing people (or giving up on them)

. . . from the wrong conclusion

. . . from missing out on all the wonderful rewards that come to those who wait.

Patience, as Edison illustrated, is a primary ingredient of genius. Even fits of inspiration or flashes of brilliance are worthless without the patience to polish, refine, and ultimately release. Edison's genius was exactly this—the patient commitment to test things over and over again, to put an experiment or an invention aside until someone could procure him better raw materials, figuring out how not just to invent the light bulb, but to doggedly develop a way of delivering the electricity underground to the first block of houses and then navigating the politics required to actually make this a reality in New York City.

It is impossible for an impatient person to work with others. It is impossible for them not to make errors of judgment and of timing. It is impossible for them to do important things, because almost everything that matters takes longer than it should, certainly longer than we would like.

Meanwhile, the patient person is not only easier to work with, but more protected and resilient. As da Vinci wrote, "Patience serves as protection against wrongs as clothes do against cold. For if you put on more clothes as the cold increases, it will have no power to hurt you. So in like manner you must grow in patience when you meet with great wrongs, and they will then be powerless to vex your mind."

Buckle up and wait. That's what it takes.

We will need not just day-to-day patience, but *long* patience. Shackleton level patience. To put the book in a drawer while it gestates, to go to sleep and come back to it tomorrow, to let the compounding interest do its work, to let your investment appreciate, to let your plan take effect, to let people catch up to your idea that was ahead of its time . . . to be vindicated by events to come.

But that's the point. If things went exactly the way we wanted, if it didn't demand discomfort and sacrifice and patient endurance, then no discipline would be required, and *everyone* would do it.

Then the fruit wouldn't just be less sweet—someone would have already eaten it.

Perfectionism Is a Vice

~

In the winter of 1931, Martha Graham was hopelessly bogged down in a dance series she had choreographed called *Ceremonials,* inspired by Mayan and Aztec cultures. A notorious perfectionist, she despaired of ever completing the dance. Worried, self-critical, consumed by guilt that she had wasted her Guggenheim Fellowship, Graham was convinced she could not meet the expectations of her rising reputation, much less the vision she had in her own head.

"The winter is lost," she whimpered in self-pity. "The whole winter's work is lost. I've destroyed my year. This work is no good."

Even though her dancers loved it, even though they had committed body and soul to it, all she could see was what needed to be changed. All she could see were the ways it wasn't perfect. And it trapped her in a kind of creative prison.

It's the tragic fate of greats across many different fields. Their success is built on their incredibly high standards—often higher than anyone, including the audience or the market, could demand—but this virtue is also a terrible vice, not just preventing them from enjoying what they have achieved, but making it increasingly impossible to ship the next thing.

Because it's never good enough. Because there's always more they can do. Because it doesn't measure up to what they did last time.

Da Vinci was like this, becoming almost serially incapable of finishing his paintings. Steve Jobs got stuck releasing the Macintosh before he was fired from Apple. A biographer of the novelist Ralph Ellison speaks of a perfectionism that was so "clogging" the man's arteries that, in one case, Ellison produced forty drafts of a short statement about one of his own books—a book he had lived and breathed for decades and should have been able to hammer out in forty *minutes.* The tragic result was that Ellison never published a follow-up to his masterpiece, *Invisible Man,* despite writing some *nineteen inches* of futile manuscript pages over the years.

What was it? Was it humility? An obsession with getting the little things right? No, those are the reassuring excuses we make for what is often a kind of narcissism and obsession. We're convinced everyone cares *so much* about what we're doing that we get stuck. We tell ourselves it's self-discipline when in fact, it's self-consciousness.

As they say, another way to spell "perfectionism" is p-a-r-a-l-y-s-i-s.

An obsession with getting it perfect misses the forest for the trees, because ultimately the biggest miss of all is failing to get your shot off. What you don't ship, what you're too afraid or strict to release, to *try*, is, by definition, a failure. It doesn't matter the cause, whether it was from procrastination or perfectionism, the result is the same. You didn't do it.

The Stoics remind us: We can't abandon a pursuit because we despair of perfecting it. Not trying because you're not sure you can win, you're not sure whether everyone will love it, there's a word for that too: *cowardice.*

We have to be brave enough to soldier on. To give it a shot. To take our turn. To step into the arena, even though we might well lose. We have to be *strong enough* to do this too.

Martha Graham was lucky to have collaborators who pushed her when necessary and helped to rescue her from the excesses of her own exacting self-discipline. When she was trapped with *Ceremonies*, her musical director, Louis Horst, stepped in and told her, "One cannot always create on the same level. The Sixth Symphony followed the Fifth, but without the Sixth we could not have had the Seventh. One cannot know what one is leading into. Transitions are as important as achievements."

Perfect is not just the enemy of the good, as they say, but it's the enemy of everything that might come after. If you get stuck, your potential does too. This is why *finishing* is itself an achievement, an act of monumental discipline that *must* happen.

Of course, you'll want to keep tinkering, keep tweaking, keep running the problems over in your mind. But you need to be able to stop yourself, to say, finally, *this is done.* And if you can't do that on your own, if you have trouble with the last mile on your projects, or if you know you can fall prey to perfectionism, then do you have the self-discipline to find partners who can cut you off and balance you out?

Martha was certainly successful enough to surround herself with sycophants and yes-men, but she didn't. She understood she needed moderating influences—wise advisors and trusted patrons—if she was to produce great work. As great as Ralph Ellison and da Vinci were, as in command of their genius as they both were, they struggled with this.

As Martha's biographer and dance partner, Agnes de Mille, explained about Louis,

> He was the one—the only one—who could discipline Martha herself into finishing her pieces, shaping them up and getting them ready for performance. He was quite practical about this. After giving her leeway for weeks, or even months he would at last call a halt and demand decisions, which Martha, in her hysterical turmoils, did not always wish to make. The dances got done—not always finished, but done.

Thanks to Louis, she wrote, *there always was a first performance.*

And without a first performance, we know, there's never a chance of moving closer to that perfect asymptote we're all striving to reach.

Do the Hard Thing First

~

There have been fewer quotes more misunderstood and misattributed than Nicholas Chamfort's suggestion that "A man must swallow a toad every morning if he wishes to be sure of finding nothing still more disgusting before the day is over."

Shortened and often credited to Mark Twain,* the idea is that if we *eat the frog* at the beginning of the day, it will be next to impossible for the day to get any worse. A more applicable interpretation of this idea was expressed by the poet and pacifist William Stafford's daily rule: "Do the hard things first."

Don't wait. Don't tell yourself you'll warm up to it. Don't tell yourself you'll get this other stuff out of the way and *then* . . .

No. Do it now.

Do it first.

That's called prioritization.

Get it over with.

---

*In fact, Chamfort himself credits an unknown M. de Lassay for the line.

That's called self-care.

Remember, Toni Morrison didn't get up before dawn for some "me time." The mornings weren't for catching up on the news or folding laundry. She had a short window and she used it to write—seizing the day while others weren't yet stirring.

This wasn't easy. There were many days where she didn't want to. But when she followed through, when she did her pages quietly in the morning light, not only was she moving closer to her goal of becoming a great writer, she was, in another sense, giving herself "me time." Because now the rest of the day was a bonus. By taking care of (difficult) business, she was taking care of herself. She had owned the morning—she had eaten the frog—and now everything else was extra. Nothing else was harder than the battle she'd already won.

Just as days are made of mornings, lives are made of days. To procrastinate at any time, day or night, young or old, *to push it until later,* is a loser's game.

The one thing all fools have in common, Seneca wrote, is that they're always getting *ready* to live. They tell themselves they just need to get some things in place first, that they're just not feeling it yet, that they'll get to it after . . .

. . . what, exactly?

Exactly *nothing.*

They never get to it. We never do.

You'll need to be smarter than that, more disciplined than that.

"I ceaselessly chant the refrain," Montaigne said, "anything you can do another day can be done now."

"He who postpones the hour of living right," Horace wrote, "is like the rustic who waits for the river to run out before he crosses."

To paraphrase the Stoics: You could be good now. Instead you chose tomorrow.

To procrastinate is to be entitled. It is arrogant. It assumes there will be a *later*. It assumes you'll have the discipline to get to it later (despite not having the discipline now).

The graveyard of lost potential, we might say, is filled with people who just needed to do something else *first*.

The time to do it is now.

The time to get started is now.

The thing to start with is the hard part, the part you want to do the least. Not begrudgingly, but promptly and enthusiastically, with a body that's been trained for hard work and a mind that's sharp and focused.

Fools are too weak, too scared, too ill-disciplined for this— which is a problem for them but an opportunity for you.

Because it's here that you'll win. They'll be delaying, you'll be pulling ahead.

But only if you start now.

Can You Get Back Up?

~

In 1959, Floyd Patterson put his title on the line to fight Ingemar Johansson.

Although he trained hard for the fight, there was something missing in Patterson's camp as the day approached. Maybe it was hunger. Maybe it was commitment.

Patterson was bored. He was impatient. He was overconfident.

And when he got in the ring, it showed. He was not the man who deserved to win. "Every fighter should be a little afraid of what could happen to him," Patterson would reflect on the fight later, "because fear makes your mind sharper. When you have nothing to fear, your mind becomes dull."

But he didn't think he could lose, and you could see he wasn't sharp.

In the third round, he went down. *Seven times.* The fight was finally stopped.

The horrible words came to him as the fog from the punches cleared. "I've lost the championship." Patterson couldn't believe it. But it was true. And more painfully still: It was all his fault.

Now, this could have been the end of the story. In fact, for all of boxing history up to that point and almost every title fight since it was. Once a champion loses their belt, they *never* win it back. They're done. They're down. For the count.

Patterson spent weeks moping, kicking himself. The guilt made him sick. He could barely sleep and or even look his children in the eye. He was knocked *out*.

Then a letter arrived from Archie Moore, the boxer who Patterson had himself beaten to get the title. "Dear Floyd," it said, "I know how you must feel. I hope you don't continue to feel bad. The same thing has happened to many fighters. Of course, I hated to lose to you, and fate decreed it that way." Continuing, the letter broke down the fight and the obvious problems with Patterson's strategy, before concluding, "If you concentrate your jab and move around this guy, you can be the first one to regain the crown. You can do it. Your friend, Archie Moore."

It's worth taking a minute to recognize the incredible kindness as well as self-discipline it takes for a former champion to take the time to write, unsolicited, such encouragement to their archnemesis at their lowest moment. Moore could have taunted Patterson; instead he helped him believe in himself.

This moment of grace was exactly what Patterson, who was slipping into despair, so badly needed. His backslide was arrested. The pity party ended. He had been reminded of his agency—*he could turn this into something.* Training camp resumed. He willed himself to watch the film of his ignominious defeat, learning from each tortuous viewing. And then in June 1960, almost exactly a year later to the day, Floyd Patterson knocked out Ingemar Johansson midway through the fifth round. Floyd hit Johansson so hard the man took five minutes to regain consciousness in the middle of the ring.

In twenty years of prizefighting, Patterson was the first ever (and only one of four since) to regain a heavyweight title—a powerful reminder that defeat is not final and that backslides can be stopped.

We're all going to mess up. We'll show up to a life-changing opportunity unprepared. We'll fall off our diet or our sobriety. We'll lose our temper and embarrass ourselves. We'll make mistakes. We'll be beaten. That's the thing about discipline: It never fails us, but sometimes we fail it.

But will that be the end of it? Is that who we are now? Or can we get back up?

Losing is not always up to us . . . but being a loser is. Being a quitter is. Saying, "Ah, what the hell, does it even matter?" That's on us. Throwing in the towel on a fight we've clearly lost is one thing, throwing in the towel on fighting, on your standards, from that point forward? Now you've been more than beaten, you've been *defeated.*

Don't be frustrated that you're not constitutionally calm or perfect. Because no one is, and no one is expecting you to be!

If your standards are so high that you give up when you fall short of them, then actually you don't have high standards. What you have are excuses.

This is another reason why that perfectionism—moral or professional—is so dangerous. When we fall short, when we are revealed as the fundamentally flawed, vulnerable, beatable, screwed-up people we are? It can be hard to get going again. If we're too hard on ourselves, as Floyd Patterson was, as Martha Graham was, we'll knock ourselves out . . . out of the fight entirely.

We are all going to screw up. We're going to relapse—on the diet, on the bad habit, whatever. We're going to blow it in public—not hustling like we should, giving in to temptation or a fit of passion, perhaps even having a moment of cowardice. We are going to lose. Nobody stays undefeated for long in this life.

And then what?

Can we gather ourselves back up? Can we regroup and try again?

It's wonderfully fitting that in both the Zen tradition and the Bible we have a version of the proverb about falling down seven times and *getting up eight* (it was also what Patterson literally did after that horrible third round).

The great home run hitter Sadaharu Oh used to say that for an athlete, losing just meant the opportunity come back tomorrow and try to do better. The same was true for winning too.

That's what being a pro is about: treating winning or losing as a chance to get right back to it. To come back to your groove and stay in it—because that's where you're happiest, most in control, most connected.

Even the most cheerful, even the strongest, even the most self-disciplined of us will stagger under the weight of our circumstances or the consequences of our behavior. We remember Viktor Frankl today as an unflagging optimist, the unwavering believer in human meaning despite the horrors he endured in the Holocaust. And yet, there is a note he sent to some friends in 1945, just after the war ended, that read:

> I am unspeakably tired, unspeakably sad, unspeakably lonely . . . In the camp, you really believed you had reached the low point of life—and then, when you came back, you were forced to see that things had not lasted, everything that had sustained you had been destroyed, that at the time when you have become human again, you could sink into an even more bottomless suffering.

It's hard to blame him. It is also unfathomable to think of what humanity would have been deprived of if he had wallowed here, or worse, given up. Instead, *in spite of everything,* he got back up. He said yes to life, to a second try, to getting back in the ring, to clawing his way back to happiness with purpose.

If he can do it, after all that, we all can.

Our self-discipline compels us to. Our destiny depends on it.

The Battle Against Pain

John F. Kennedy may have been born handsome and rich, but he was not dealt a good hand by the gods. He had a distant, imperious father and was born into a family with a history of addiction. His body was a source of continual trouble. From ulcers to Addison's disease to a degenerative back problem—exacerbated first by football, then by war injuries—Kennedy was in almost constant pain. And his traumatic childhood and difficult job only added stress and tension on top.

This was not his fault.

Beyond frustrating, it was excruciating. He must have lain there in bed some mornings—or other times on the floor, when he had fallen—and wondered if it was worth getting up.

Yet one cannot help but read Kennedy's medical history and be terrified at the lengths he was willing to go for relief. As president, he took corticosteroids, procaine, Lomotil, testosterone, paregoric, phenobarbital, penicillin, amphetamines, and anything else he could get his hands on. He once told the British prime minister that if he didn't have sex constantly, he'd get migraines.

When one doctor saw the injectable cocktail of amphetamines and painkillers Kennedy was taking, he tried to intervene. "I don't care if it's horse piss," Kennedy replied. "It works."

Did it?

Because Kennedy constantly needed more and more and more.

He doctor shopped, allowing a parade of shady practitioners into his life (and the Oval Office), despite the warnings from people who knew better. Inevitably, the medications took their toll on Kennedy. He was still in pain. He became depressed. He felt like was trying to think through a fog. But instead of weaning himself off, he doubled down, getting a prescription for Stelazine, an incredibly strong antipsychotic.

History rightly celebrates Kennedy for his calm, wise temperance in the tense thirteen days of the Cuban Missile Crisis, but a closer inspection shows us the daily danger his medical recklessness placed upon millions and millions of people. "No president with his finger on the red button has any business taking stuff like that," a doctor warned him when he heard about the Stelazine, threatening to go to the press if Kennedy didn't stop taking it immediately.

That's the thing about both pain and pleasure: They're felt in the body, but they affect the mind and the mood—*our temperament*—which is something we must protect always.

Are there acceptable drugs and treatments out there? Of course.

No one should think that getting help for depression or for chronic pain is somehow contrary to the principles of temperance. Epictetus suffered all his life from a leg twisted and broken by torture—if there had been a safe way to moderate this pain, he'd have been stupid not to explore it. And we will find ourselves in positions like that. We'll have accidents. Our bodies will age. Our hearts will be broken.

The problem is that Kennedy hoped a magic pill (or *pills*) would make his problems go away. He used sex and medicine as an escape, not as a tool. The pain wasn't his fault, but the bad decisions he made to get rid of it were.

In fact, the one treatment that actually did something about his back pain was quite simple. The doctor who objected to Kennedy's drug use found that the president could not do a single sit-up. "You will be a cripple soon if you don't start exercising," he explained to Kennedy. "Five days a week. And you need to start now." With stretching and breathing exercises, weights, and then calisthenics, Kennedy regained much of his mobility. The pain levels dropped to something more manageable. "I wish I could have known you ten years ago," Kennedy told the doctor. It looked like he'd even be able to stop using his back brace.*

---

* The one he was wearing when he was assassinated, which made him a particularly fixed target.

While not every problem can be solved with fresh air and exercise, we must be very suspicious of anyone who tells us they can make our pain disappear without real work. Dr. Feelgoods (as one of Kennedy's doctors was called) are like Sirens of Greek myth: Their song is sweet . . . but often deadly.

Yet generation after generation ignores this fact. Today, without irony, people (in considerably less pain—physically at least) have popularized the phrase *doing the work* to describe their use of all sorts of experimental psychedelic drugs to address their spiritual or mental malaise. They say this even as a fentanyl epidemic ravages and kills those around them, as the world staggers from the consequences of an opioid crisis.

Medicine is not something to play with!

Pope John Paul II was right to remind us that part of temperance is about avoiding the impulse to deprive ourselves of "consciousness by the use of drugs." Our rational faculties (as well as our bodies) can torture us, but they are also a gift. We ought not dull their power or mess, unnecessarily, with our chemistry.

Doing the work? The *work* is getting through life sober. Go on a trip? Go to therapy! Struggle with it. Heal a little bit each day, get a little better each day.

Perhaps that's why the path that Kennedy got on is so seductive—believing that there is just some single thing that can unlock our relief, some Soma-like pill or device that can save us from pain or boredom or despair. In fact, it's this very hope that makes us vulnerable to gurus or doctors who prey on people in agony. Anyone or anything that offers you an escape should be viewed with caution and anything that promises *euphoria* liable to give you real pain.

"Doing the work" must actually mean thinking about things holistically. It must mean getting to the root causes. It should mean solving for the injury, not the symptoms. It means therapy—in Kennedy's case, not just the physical therapy, but the desperate need for psychological help too. This will take real courage as well as self-discipline. Because it takes longer. Because it means facing scary things, because it means inching our way to progress, not instant transformation. This will not be easy. But the side effects are at least minimal.

It may also mean, no matter how unfair or unpleasant it is, finding a way to *live with* pain.

The Stoics had a word for this, *emmenetea*—what must be tolerated. Lou Gehrig knew that a long career in baseball would require playing hurt, as life itself demands. "I remember when Lou had a broken middle finger on his right hand," one teammate recalled. "Every time he batted a ball it hurt him. And he almost got sick to his stomach when he caught the ball. You could see him wince. But he always stayed in the game." At 2,044 games, he was hit with a crippling case of lumbago, which sends sharp pains through the lower back and makes standing up straight a challenge. Would this be the end? "I'll shake it off," Gehrig replied. "That's what I've always done." He could have turned back to drink or worse . . . but he didn't. He stayed clean. He stayed in the game.

But pain can also be an indicator, a warning light, a reminder to slow down or make a change. That's why Gregg Popovich was willing to take the fine for resting his players—better financial pain than painful injuries (and painkillers). For too long, Kennedy wasn't interested in fixing what was wrong, only in finding a way to continue—his affairs, his youth, his denial of his limitations—despite the danger.

His body tried to warn him. His doctors tried to warn him.

He ignored them.

Queen Elizabeth is as tough as they get. But you don't make it that long without listening to your body, without taking care of yourself. She's relied on sustainable practices, not shortcuts. As she advised a young wife of a diplomat who ached after the long days of standing without break, "One must plant their feet like this. Always keep them parallel. Make sure your weight is evenly distributed. That's all there is to it."

There's more to it, of course, but it's a start.

We endure pain, but we also have to address the root causes of it.

The mind and the body must find a way to work together, temperately, moderately, soberly.

The Battle Against Pleasure

Epicurus was supposedly a pleasure-addicted hedonist. The inscription above the man's garden does lend itself to that impression. "Stranger, here you will do well to tarry," it said, "here our highest good is pleasure. The caretaker of that abode, a kindly host, will be ready for you; he will welcome you with bread, and serve you water also in abundance, with these words: 'Have you not been well entertained? This garden does not whet your appetite, but quenches it.'"

What kind of pleasure was he promising?

Food?

Sex?

Drink?

Debauchery?

Few people in third century BC Athens were sure, so they assumed the worst. Here, thousands of years later, we perpetuate their suspicions, loosely defining an "Epicurean" as a person who indulges every sensual urge.

Anyone who actually reads Epicurus's philosophy, though, finds a much simpler prescription for happiness. In one famous letter, Epicurus, talking to a rich friend who promised him anything he wanted, requested a small pot of cheese with which to treat himself. "Such was the man," wrote the ancient biographer Diogenes Laërtius, "who laid down that *pleasure was the end of life.*"

To Epicurus, pleasure was not gluttony. It was not mindlessly giving the body whatever it ached for.

"By pleasure," Epicurus said, "we mean the absence of pain in the body and of trouble in the mind. It is not an unbroken succession of drinking-bouts and of merrymaking, not the satisfaction of lusts, not the enjoyment of the fish and other delicacies of a luxurious table, which produce a pleasant life; it is sober reasoning, searching out the motives of every choice and avoidance, and banishing those beliefs through which the greatest disturbances take possession of the soul."

Epicurus was no King George IV, nor would he have wanted to be, as it was not particularly pleasurable to be King George. Not only did the man's gluttony cut his life short, but allowing himself everything he wanted turned quite quickly into a daily nightmare. How much fun was Babe Ruth having when they had to rush him to the hospital stuffed sick with food and booze?

We don't refrain from excess because it's a sin. We are self-disciplined because we want to avoid a hellish existence right here while we're alive—a hell of our own making.

The body is stupid, you have to understand, and our temperament has to save it from itself. The body wants to eat until it is full . . . but it ends up way past that point. The body wants to drink until it is drunk . . . but we only feel that way when we're well beyond drunk. The body wants to be numb . . . it can put up with horse piss if it works, as Kennedy said. The body wants what it wants now . . . it can deal with the consequences later. We have to be smart and self-controlled and *self-aware* enough to intervene before that happens. And for [eating more than we should] you can insert just about anything we are prone to take to excess, from drinking to working to having fun to staying up late. As Timotheus, the Athenian statesman, once said after a delightful party at Plato's house, "Your dinners are enjoyable not only when one is eating them but on the morning after as well!" If you're stuffed and uncomfortable afterward, if you're hungover and groggy when you wake up, if you're filled with regret or shame, or you don't even remember what happened the night before, was it really that great in the first place?

The Stoics said that this was a perfect metaphor for everything we do. "Remember to conduct yourself in life as if at a banquet," Epictetus said. "As something being passed around comes to you, reach out your hand and take a moderate helping. Does it pass you by? Don't stop it. It hasn't yet come? Don't burn in desire for it, but wait until it arrives in front of you. Act this way with children, a spouse, toward position, with wealth—one day it will make you worthy of a banquet with the gods."*

"Always remember," Churchill once reassured his wife, "that I have taken more out of alcohol than alcohol has taken out of me." This is a critical test. Don't just think about what a certain pleasure will give, think about what it will take out of you. Think about how what you're chasing is going to age. Think about how you'll think about it *after*—during the refractory period, during your hangover, when your pants are too tight, when you catch yourself in the mirror months from now and wonder *how this happened.*

Of course, abstinence and restraint are not the same thing. One is about avoidance, the other is about responsibility. It's understanding how to do these things appropriately—for your body, for your genetics, for your lifestyle. Temperance, C. S. Lewis reminds us, is about "going to the right length and no further."

As Musonius Rufus reminds us, that "by the standard of pleasure, nothing is more pleasant than self-control and . . . nothing is more painful than lack of self-control." Nobody who has given themselves over to excess is having a good time. No one enslaved to their appetites is free.

---

* Of course, for some people and some things, the appropriate amount *is* none. See "Quit Being a Slave."

The ability to rise from the table before the point of hating yourself, before the meat sweats or the carb coma—this takes strength. So does nursing one drink through dinner instead of going back for more or stopping only at the signs of impairment. And so is knowing, finally, that a bigger house isn't going to make you happier, that you don't need more money, more fans, more *anything.* Never approaching, let alone passing, the point of regret while still enjoying things that are fun, that make you happy, that give you pleasure. Recognizing that your choices have put you in a dangerous fog, as Kennedy couldn't do. This takes self-knowledge, self-control, and—if the people around you seem ready to keep the party going—no small amount of courage.

Discipline is not a punishment, it's a way to avoid punishment. We do it because we love ourselves, we value ourselves and what we do. And we find, conveniently enough, that it also heightens our enjoyment of things as well. Indeed, the person content with less, who can enjoy a small pot of cheese as if it were a culinary bounty, is much more easily satisfied and much better able to find good in all situations.

Seek yourself, not distraction.

Be happy, not hedonistic.

Let the mind rule, not the body.

Conquer pleasure, make yourself superior to pain.

Fight the Provocation

$\sim$

Arthur Ashe's father was working one day as a driver for William Thalhimer, a wealthy Jewish man in Richmond, Virginia, who owned a chain of department stores. Taking his boss across town to see about a piece of real estate he wanted to buy, Arthur Ashe Sr. was given a firsthand look at the kind of discrimination that Jews also faced in the un-Reconstructed South in the 1950s.

Throughout the negotiation, Thalhimer was insulted, condescended to, and bullied by a man who seemed to be particularly disgusted at the thought of doing business with a Jew. Quietly enduring it, Thalhimer completed the transaction and he and Ashe Sr. got back in the car to drive home.

Why? Ashe couldn't help but ask. *Why did you put up with all that?*

"I came out here to purchase that piece of land," Thalhimer explained. "I got the piece of land. It belongs to me now, not to him. That man can go on cursing me as long as he likes. I have that land."

Of course, he had wanted to slam his fist in the man's face, but that would have given the anti-Semite exactly what he wanted, right? To not have to do business with a Jew? And where would that have left Thalhimer? Without the land he wanted. Quite possibly in jail.

With the distance afforded by the passage of time, we can appreciate both the injustice of what occurred and marvel at the quiet dignity and self-control exhibited by Thalhimer in this moment. Certainly Ashe Sr., a black man in the segregated South, would have acutely appreciated both things. In fact, his son, Arthur Ashe Jr., would note that it was this experience that shaped his father as a provider and inspired him, during segregation, to always be pragmatic as well as patient and self-contained. Ashe Sr. didn't care what people said about him or did to him. What mattered was supporting his family and setting his two sons up for success in a world that seemed very much intent on them not being successful. Racists be damned, Arthur Ashe Sr. was going to *get that land.*

Obviously, it would be wonderful if this didn't have to happen. If no one was ever subjected to slurs or discrimination, if everyone were kind to us, if we were never deprived, judged, assaulted, or treated shabbily. But that is not life.

There is a story about Cato the Younger, the great-grandson of the frugal Roman Cato the Elder, who was visiting the baths in Rome one day, when he was bumped and then struck in one of those random encounters that seem to combust into a full-on fight when you come across somebody who is *just having a bad day*. But once the scuffle had broken up and Cato could collect himself, he simply refused to accept an apology from the offender, though not in the way one might expect. "I don't even remember being hit," he said. Beyond refusing the apology, he declined to carry a grudge too.

James Peck, one of the only white Freedom Riders, would note several times how his refusal to retaliate would stun his attackers into a momentary lull and, one might imagine, a terrifying moment of self-reflection. *Why isn't this person consumed with hatred like I am? Why aren't they out of control like me? Are they actually* better *than me?*

Remember always: As wrong as they are, as annoying as it is, it takes two for a real conflict to happen. As the Stoics said, when we are offended, when we fight, we are complicit. We have *chosen* to engage. We have traded self-control for self-indulgence. We've allowed our cooler head to turn hot—even though we know hot heads rarely make good decisions.

Life . . . people . . . they're going to give you the opportunity. You can decline to accept it.

Aesop's old fable about the lion buzzed about and stung by a gnat? We have to develop the ability to ignore, to endure, to forget. Not just cruel provocations from jerks, but also unintentional slights and mistakes from people we love or respect, lest we do more damage to ourselves than the sting of those slights ever could.

"It helps to be a little deaf," was the advice that Ruth Bader Ginsburg was given by her mother-in-law, and it helped guide her through not just fifty-six years of marriage, but also a twenty-seven-year career on the Supreme Court with colleagues she adored but surely disagreed with on a regular basis, not least of whom was Antonin Scalia, her best friend and ideological opposite.

Think of what Ginsburg and Ashe Sr. and Thalhimer had to endure. During periods in history when laws and social mores were almost never on their side. And you're struggling not to freak out in response to what is literally called a *micro*aggression? C'mon.

We can pretend to not see it. We can ignore what they said about us on the email chain to which we were cc'd. We don't have to assume the worst. We don't have to turn the buzzing gnat into a national referendum. We don't have to let it rattle us.

Why should you have to, though?

Because you have work to do. They *want* you to get upset. Because if you're going to stop and reply to every attack, as Lincoln said, you might as well admit defeat right now. You'll never get anything done. You'll certainly never be happy. And they'll have won.

It's the easiest thing in the world to respond to intemperance with intemperance. We have to remember: Someone else's lack of self-control is not a justification for abandoning our own. Nor is it a good look or a recipe for success and achievement.

Arthur Ashe Jr. learned that self-control from his father, which he in turn had seen so powerfully embodied in William Thalhimer.

His destiny as a tennis player—as your own destiny will be—was reached by channeling the provocations of life productively. He showed up and did what he came to do on the court.

Nothing. No distractions. No setbacks.

Nothing could stop him.

Beware This Madness

~

In Game 7 of the 2004 Western Conference Semifinals, Sam Cassell hit an incredible shot from the corner to give the Minnesota Timberwolves a two-point lead. It was one of those shots that only the best athletes can possibly hope to make, under the kind of pressure that very few will ever possibly know.

Which is why the cameras and the crowd loved what happened next: As Cassell transitioned back on defense, carried away with excitement and pride, his arms hanging down between his legs like a cradle, he took triumphant, pounding strides, motioning as if he was straining to carry his enormous testicles.

It also happened that, in the midst of this famous Big Balls dance, Cassell created a small avulsion fracture in his hip. As a result, the Timberwolves, the number one seed with home-court advantage throughout the playoffs, fell to the Lakers in the conference finals in six games. Cassell, limited by the injury, was barely a factor.

Of course, in the calm and mild light of hindsight, no one

would trade an NBA championship for a few seconds of celebration or taunting, but that's the thing about a fit of passion.

It blinds us.

It carries us away. It overrides our judgment. It makes it impossible to be patient. To bite our tongue. To resist temptation. To ignore a slight.

Oh, what this costs us. Oh, what we come to regret.

Sometimes it's a moment of arrogance or excitement. Or anger. Or anxiety. Or avarice. Or envy.

Or lust...

Think of the powerful men (and women) whose careers were derailed by a sex scandal. They had power, they had influence, the future was bright. What would possess them to risk it all for some fleeting pleasure? Why would someone as brave and decent as Martin Luther King Jr. cheat on his wife in those squalid hotel rooms? The philosopher Democritus wasn't wrong when he described sex as a "mild madness." It makes us crazy. It makes us do shameful things.

Anger is just a slightly less mild form of madness. Whom the gods destroy, they first make mad, said another philosopher. Lincoln's famous "hot letters" were the things he wrote in anger but was disciplined enough to send to a drawer in his desk and not the deserving recipient. On the other hand, the most pointless scandals of Truman's presidency were the mean notes he sent, including one to a critic at the *New York Times* who had written negatively about his daughter. A generally self-disciplined president, these missives, these uninhibited blasts of passion, were uncharacteristic. Alas, anger got the best of one of the best of us.

Nearly every regret, every mistake, every embarrassing moment—whether it be personal or professional or historical—have one thing in common: Somebody lost control of their emotions. Somebody got carried away. Somebody was scared, or defensive. Somebody wasn't thinking beyond the next few seconds.*

That's the irony of our obsession with talking so positively about "passion" these days. The ancients had precisely the opposite view of the word. *The passions* were considered very dangerous. Something to beware of. Because even when they were positive—which they often were not—they tended to lead us astray. To hijack our minds or our bodies, and sometimes both. We codify this even into our legal system, referring to *crimes of passion.*

If you cannot rein in your impulses now, if you can be jerked like a puppet today, how do you think it will go when you reach the level you aspire to? When you have power, when you have people willing to make excuses for you, when you have resources? And, too, when the margin for error is also much smaller?

---

* "Drinking is the kindling wood of passion," St. Ambrose pointed out. A lack of self-discipline when it comes to drugs and alcohol makes it harder to be self-disciplined with our emotions or decisions.

People who are doing less important things than you can get away with not being in control. You can't.

You can't afford for a moment of ego or excitement costing yourself (and your teammates) a championship. You can't afford for an impulse decision to undermine your training. You can't afford to let passion block out the calm and mild light.

Maybe other people can. Not you.

Does that mean you never get to be spontaneous or to let out your emotions? Of course not. Love and be loved—feel passion. The idea is to stop yourself from saying something cruel to that person you love when you're upset . . . or betray the trust of the person you love because of a few seconds of temptation. You can get angry . . . the important thing is *not to do anything out of anger.*

And for [anger] we can plug in so many other emotions we feel passionately in the moment.

John Wooden tried to keep the passion on his team to a minimum. He found it to be an unsustainable and dangerous fuel. "I wanted them bristling with intensity, finely focused, and in control of themselves," he said. "When these attitudes are combined with talent and good teaching, you may find yourself leading a team competing and prevailing at the highest levels. This will not occur if you are a slave to passion."

Of all the bad habits to quit, passion is the hardest one. Because it happens in bursts. Because it's such powerful and combustible fuel. Because before we even recognize we're in the sway of it, the damage is done. We can have passion, but no one can afford to be a *slave* to it.

The key is to slow things down. Think things through. Try not to be driven by forces you don't understand or control. Just as an addict looks for the warning signs of a craving, we must look for insertion points for our self-discipline before we get carried away. Whether it's anxiety or aggression, lust for a person or a thing, a celebration or an overwhelming uncertainty, we must step in and pull the emergency brake before the urge to act on those emotions picks up so much steam that it crashes us into a wall.

Always, always take the exit ramp when it presents itself.

There's a story about Queen Elizabeth, who, after a long day of travel with her late husband, Prince Philip, found him worked up and in an argument. The Queen, saving him from himself, caught her husband's attention and pointed out the display in front of them. "Look at the pottery," she said calmly and slowly. Shaken out of his fit, Philip stopped and looked, bringing himself back to a state of royal dignity. Later, a politician who had overheard the exchange would walk over to the scene where it had occurred. He was only half surprised to find there had never been any pottery at all.

When you've planned a thing that's wrong—as the famous Mr. Rogers lyric goes—you must stop and do something else instead. When you see someone about to give themselves over to a fit of passion, see if you can't help them redirect that energy.

Because we're in charge. Our training. Our teaching. Our talent. Our (good!) temperament. They are our guide. They take the lead.

Not our passions.

Not the momentary mild (or not so mild) madness.

Silence Is Strength

~

It's so easy to marvel at the courage of the Spartans that we often miss their other feats of strength.

Told that Xerxes's arrows would blot out the sun, Leonidas replied, "Then we shall fight in the shade." Told by another conqueror that if his army breached their walls, he'd slaughter every single soldier, the Spartans replied with one word, *"If . . ."*

Obviously these retorts—made in the face of death—took real *cojones*. It's also unquestionable that the Spartans *laconic* style (which is named after them) is part and parcel of their culture of self-discipline. They never used two words where one would do. They never said more than was necessary—never shot off at the mouth, never overshared, never droned on or bloviated.

As Archimedes once explained at a Spartan dinner, "An expert on speaking also knows when not to do so." The Spartans kept their tongues in check, even when it meant that some people might think less of them. In a big argument, one Spartan listened but said nothing. Are you stupid? someone asked. "Well, certainly a stupid person wouldn't be able to keep quiet," he replied. And of one famous Spartan it was said that it was impossible to "find a man who knew more but spoke less."

Robert Greene puts it perfectly: "Powerful people impress and intimidate by saying less."

The irony, of course, is that with power comes license to say whatever you what, whenever you want, to whomever you want. And yet, it is the discipline to *not* do these thing that creates the presence that powerful people enjoy.

It isn't easy to do. Especially today. Not only does the ego want to talk, want to say what it thinks, but now we have technology that exploits ego and explicitly tempts you to share, to speak, to get in pointless arguments, to burst out with hot takes.

Online or in person, we can't just sit there. We jump in because we think we're supposed to. We jump in because we don't want to seem dumb (even though by speaking we risk removing all doubt). We jump in *because we just can't live with someone else being wrong and not knowing it.*

Where does this get us? Usually into trouble. Rarely does it make any sort of positive difference. Never does it help us with our *main thing*. It's almost always a distraction from that main thing!

Can you . . .

- keep a secret?
- bite your tongue about someone or something you dislike?

- get someone else to deliver the news?
- put up with being misunderstood?

It's a balance. While each of us needs to cultivate the courage to speak up and speak the truth, we also need to develop the self-discipline to know when to stay focused and when to shut up (and how to measure what we do say with the utmost economy).

You don't have to verbalize every thought. You don't have to always give your opinion—especially when it's not solicited. Just because there is a pause doesn't mean you have to fill it. Just because everyone else is talking doesn't mean you have to jump in. You can sit with the awkwardness. You can use the silence to your advantage. You can wait and see.

You can decide not to speak through words at all . . . and let your work speak for you.

Angela Merkel famously uses almost no adjectives in her speeches, but when she speaks, you listen, because you know that every word is there for a reason. Cato chose to speak only when he was certain that his words weren't better left unsaid. Better to be thought foolish or simple than to make a fool of yourself—to prove that you don't actually have anything to say. Regret what you didn't say, not the other way around.

To be imprecise with language, to fall prey to what they now call "semantic creep"—exaggerating and misusing important words until they have no meaning—this is the mark of not just a sloppy thinker but a bad temperament. When you talk, it should matter. When you say something, it should mean something.

Remember: Free speech is a right, not an obligation. *Two ears, one mouth*, Zeno would remind his students. *Respect that ratio properly.*

Let them wish you talked more. Let them wonder what you're thinking. Let the words you speak carry extra weight precisely because they are rare.

You can answer the question with, "I don't know." You can ignore the insult. You can decline the invitation. You can decide not to explain your reasons. You can allow for a pause. You can put it down in your journal instead. You can listen. You can sit with the silence. You can let your actions do the talking.

You can listen more than you talk. You can speak only when you're certain it's not better left unsaid.

Of course, you *can*. But *will* you?

Hold, Hold Your Fire

~

How badly Churchill must have wanted to attack.

A lifetime of *pushing,* as he had once described his ambition to lead and be at the center of things, was now intersecting with years of warnings about the menace of Nazism.

Churchill had been out of power for a decade. He had been hoping, dreaming, scheming for this moment.

Now it was his.

The Germans had overrun the French in the early summer of 1940, and now the French leadership were pleading with the British to throw the Royal Air Force into the mix. Italy, sensing French defeat, had just joined the fight and declared war on both of them. A world war had arrived. "Here is the decisive point," Maxime Weygand, the Supreme Commander of all the French forces, pleaded with Churchill at a meeting outside Paris. They were down to their "last quarter of an hour." "The British ought not to keep a single fighter in England," Churchill heard him say. "They should all be sent to France." To a man of boldness and daring, a man who had predicted this terrible scenario, newly ensconced with all the power of a prime minister, this must have been an urgent, and momentous, opportunity.

Would he rush into the fray?

No, he would not.

"This is not the decisive point," Churchill replied, after pausing to reflect, balancing courage and self-discipline and his foreboding sense of a long, hard road ahead of them. "This is not the decisive moment. The decisive moment will come when Hitler hurls his Luftwaffe against Britain. If we can keep the command of the air over our Island—that is all I ask—then we will win it all back for you . . . Whatever happens here, we are resolved to fight on for ever and ever and ever."

Almost every part of him must have wanted to say yes. All the pressure was directed at him to do it—millions of lives hung in the balance, and untold destruction too. And yet, he gathered up the quiet fortitude to rebuff an ally, to deny them what must have felt like their last and only hope, and to save his planes for the Battle of Britain—a decision that history proved more than correct.

Could you have done this? Can you trust yourself enough to stand alone? Can you stoically endure the criticism and the questioning to persist in what you know is right? Even at great cost?

A leader who cannot do this . . . well, they're not a leader. They're a follower.

At nearly every juncture of the war, Churchill was provoked.

There was always the impulse, the pressure to *do something.* From his allies. From the British people. From the enemy.

Yet success—as most strategy does—depended on judicious restraint.

In 1942 and 1943, pressure built for an Allied landing in Europe, opening the so-called second front against the Germans. Again, Churchill resisted. Taking one American diplomat on a midnight tour of Parliament, which had already been heavily bombed, Churchill explained why he had to oppose rushing in. "When I look across the well of this house," he said, "I see the faces that should be here. I'm just a sport because my contemporaries are dead. They're dead at the Passchendaele or the Somme. And we can't endure the decimation of another British generation."

Politically, supporting an invasion was the easier thing. The troops wanted it. The people wanted it. But Churchill was haunted by visions of dead British soldiers floating in the surf of France's beaches, stuck facedown in the muck of Belgium's wetlands. He knew they would get only one chance to land on the continent— this wasn't something that could be botched. He held off the forceful entreaties from his allies for nearly two full years, not because he was afraid to fight but because he knew his troops needed more time to practice and prepare. In fact, that's what the landings in Italy in September 1943 would prove—both of which were costly demonstrations of and priceless training for how difficult a successful invasion of France would be.

On June 6, 1944, the Allies landed at Normandy, with the British Second Army, including more than sixty thousand troops, leading the entire eastern flank of the invasion. This was it. With intense focus and remarkable self-discipline, Churchill had done more than wait for the right moment . . . he had *made the moment right*.

Our drive prods us. FOMO dogs us. Doubts torture us. Everyone else has already jumped in. What if we miss our moment? To resist this pressure requires real mental discipline. Sometimes we have to raise our hand, not to give the signal to go ahead, but to wait, wait, *wait for it.**

Wait for the absolute bottom (or top) of the market, even as everyone shouts that you're crazy, that you're stupid, but you know it's not quite time. Wait for the perfect job for your talents, as you turn down the promotion or hold out in contract negotiations to get what you know you're actually worth. Wait until you see the whites of their eyes . . .

Resist the bait your competitor is putting in front of you, luring them into a trap of your own. Resist the temptation to interrupt your opponent as they hang themselves. Put the time in on something classic or transgressive or shatteringly bold, even as you miss out on capitalizing on present trends that everyone insists are the future. Rest early in the season as the

---

* Or perhaps wait long enough to think better of the enterprise, as the failed invasion at the Bay of Pigs would so instruct John F. Kennedy.

Spurs did, so you can peak at the exact right moment. Wait, wait, wait for your reserves . . . so you can mount an attack that will actually succeed.

There is an old idea that goes all the way back to the Stoics but was wonderfully expressed by the English poet John Dryden: Beware the fury of the patient man.

It was hard for Churchill precisely because he was furious. He was a *doer*. He had his back against the wall. But instead, through the calm and mild light of strategic brilliance, he waited. He held his fire. And when he did take his shot, it blew the target apart.

This isn't lying to yourself about how someday, hopefully, *maybe* you'll do something. No, you've decided to act. Now you've got the harder hurdle to clear: holding on. Taking the hits while you do so, while you move with deliberateness, to get it right and make it count.

Will you?

In life, in war, in business, we often only get one moment, one opportunity. Nobody is going to give you a do-over. You never get to go back and try it differently—to make up for deficiencies in preparation, to time things better, to get more leverage.

One shot.

Are we strong enough to wait for it? Can we discipline those nerves? Can we make it *count*?

Yes. Yes, we can.

We must.

Temper Your Ambition

～

In 1791, a young Napoleon entered an essay contest with the hopes of winning its 1,200 franc prize. The prompt was a powerful one: "What are the Most Important Truths and Feelings for Men to Learn to Be Happy?"

The essay took him six months to write, and he did not win, but at age twenty-two, in his youthful excitement, he put down as good a warning about insatiable ambition as there ever was.

"What is Alexander [the Great] doing when he rushes from Thebes into Persia and thence into India? He is ever restless, he loses his wits, he believes himself God," the future conqueror would write. "What is the end of Cromwell? He governs England. But is he not tormented by all the daggers of the Furies?"

Damning illustrations of the heights on intemperance. And if that weren't enough, Napoleon then moves in for the coup de grâce, with a pronouncement whose meaning is unmistakable:

Ambition, which overthrows governments and private fortunes, which feeds on blood and crimes, ambition . . . is, like all inordinate passions, a violent and unthinking fever that ceases only when life ceases—like a conflagration which, fanned by a pitiless wind, ends only after all has been consumed.

If only the adult Napoleon had been reminded of these words. During those turbulent, destructive years when he named himself emperor of the French and mandated pompous titles like *monseigneur, altesse sérénissime* (serene highness), and *excellence* for himself while placing his incompetent relatives on thrones across Europe, if only someone could have reminded him of his own feelings about the perils of unchecked ambition . . .*

But wait, someone actually did!

In the early 1800s, Talleyrand, his foreign minister, dug up the essay in the archives and gave it to Napoleon as both a gift and a warning, which His Imperial and Royal Majesty (yet another title he gave himself) refused to accept as either. The author deserved to be whipped, Napoleon said of his younger self. "What ridiculous things I said, and how annoyed I would be if

---

*It was not a coincidence that Napoleon's physical discipline abandoned him around this time, which is why even the most flattering portrait artists could not ignore his increasing rotundness.

they were preserved," he exclaimed as he threw what he thought was the only copy into a fire.

A short time later, he would once again litter the continent with a generation of bodies and find himself exiled to a rock in the ocean where he could do no more damage to humanity.

For much of history, Alexander was the cautionary tale for unfettered ambition. Sure, he was brilliant. Sure, he accomplished incredible things. But where did it leave him? Empty. Alone. Unhappy. "Go!" he found himself taunting his own men when they finally realized he would never be satisfied. "Go tell your countrymen that you left Alexander completing the conquest of the world."

Except he died almost immediately after, and his empire collapsed with him. The poet Juvenal remarked that the whole world had not been big enough to contain Alexander . . . but in the end, a coffin was sufficient.

And what had it all been for? Like Napoleon, it hadn't been about his people or about a cause. He had waged wars of offense and aggression entirely for himself. This was a pathological need to achieve, for which the consequences were ultimately borne by basically everyone else.

There is a considerable amount of self-discipline required to quit bad habits, particularly the more gluttonous ones. But of all the addictions in the world, the most intoxicating and the hardest to control is ambition. Because unlike drinking, society rewards it. We look up to the successful. We don't ask them what they are doing or why they are doing it, we only ask them how they do it. We conveniently ignore how little satisfaction their accomplishments bring them, how miserable most of them are, and how miserable they tend to make everyone around them in turn.

Seneca, a man whose ambition got him into trouble like Napoleon, would say of a ruthless general named Marius (the Napoleon of his time) that while "Marius commanded armies, ambition commanded Marius." He lamented the leaders and businesspeople and conquerors who disrupted and disturbed the world, while they themselves were disturbed and disrupted. Marius and Napoleon and Alexander were powerful . . . but ultimately powerless. Because they couldn't stop. Because there was never enough. They lusted for control over millions, because they lacked control over themselves.

Just as we do with our relationship to drugs or devices, we have to ask ourselves: Who is in charge? Our mind? Or our slavish need to be the biggest, the winningest, the richest, the most powerful, the most famous? The need to do more, to get more, to achieve again and again? We have to ask: What is this really bringing me? What am I actually getting out of it?

Did Napoleon's accomplishments make him happy? Power and wealth didn't even make him secure! Besides the guilt and shame, which he clearly deserved, he died alone on his second island in the middle of the ocean!

Now, this criticism doesn't mean that all accomplishments

are to be scorned. What would the world look like if nobody tried to do anything? If nobody pushed to get better or do more? If we didn't have ambition—some big goal we are after—how would we know what little things, what distractions, to say no to?

Ambition is good, it just must be *tempered*. Like all elements of self-discipline, it's about balance. The monk or the priest who tries to reduce their needs to nothing, who rejects everyone and everything in pursuit of spiritual perfection, is not all that dissimilar to the billionaire who keeps building and building, or the quarterback who can't even consider retiring. At the same time, the person who dreams of nothing, who believes in nothing, who tries nothing? Well, that's not really the point either.

What we're talking about here is really temperament. We must have a sense of self and worth that can check our ceaseless ambition before it "o'erleaps itself," as Shakespeare warned.

Without the brake that prevents us from getting carried away, ambition not only deprives us of happiness, but it can very well destroy us . . . and harm others, as the insatiable conquerors invariably do, whether it's innocent victims of the wars they wage, the people they use and discard on the way up the ladder, family they neglect in the process, or the countless imitators they inspire.

We don't need accomplishments to feel good or to be good enough. What do we need?

The truth: not much!

Some food and water. Work that we can challenge ourselves with. A calm mind in the midst of adversity. Sleep. A solid routine. A cause we are committed to. Something we're getting better at.

Everything else is extra. Or worse, as history has shown countless times, the source of our painful downfall.

Money Is a (Dangerous) Tool

~

B abe Ruth made more money as an athlete than a person could have reasonably spent in a lifetime. And yet, there he was, making a pretty good go at it.

His rookie salary of six hundred dollars—when a loaf of bread cost five cents—was doled out in fifty-dollar paychecks twice a month. When Ruth received his first paycheck, he spent it on a bicycle. When he moved into the big money, it was sports cars, custom suits, leather coats, silk shirts, diamond horseshoe tie pins, and frequent trips to casinos and racetracks. When there were rumors that his marriage was in trouble, Ruth bought his first wife a five-thousand-dollar mink coat. When the Yankees clinched the pennant in 1928, Ruth rented out four rooms and threw a party at a hotel. When he learned the hotel didn't have a piano, Ruth went and bought one. His baseball salary earned him more than the president of the United States, but he'd usually start spring training borrowing from teammates until his game checks came in. "He had no idea whatsoever of money," one manager said. "He didn't seem to think it would ever run out. He'd buy anything and everything."

It was with great laughter that the Yankees locker room heard Ruth tell a young Gehrig, "Save your money . . . a bird has to think of a time when he can't play ball no longer," for it was estimated that Babe had, by that time, blown hundreds of thousands of dollars of career earnings on the high life.

He had fun along the way, more fun than a frugal man like Cato, probably. But he also came to regret it (as did his heirs) as much as his gluttony.

So many "rich" people find themselves in this position. The point of success was supposed to be security and freedom and contentment. In reality, it brought them anxiety, envy, and instability.

"The only thing that worries me in life is money," Churchill once confessed to his brother. Unlike most of the British upper class, Churchill did work for a living—becoming one of the highest-paid writers in the world. But that mattered little when he was, as his mother described him, "a perfect sieve as regard to money."

He earned it quickly and spent it faster, then wondered where it all went. His beloved Chartwell, an estate in the English countryside, was such an impulsive and ill-considered purchase, it almost cost him his marriage. Churchill would lose fifty thousand dollars speculating in the market in 1929. It was a terrible loss he could not begin to afford, but also from which he learned nothing. Promptly returning to the market, he lost three thousand in a single month on Montgomery Ward stock. And that was on top of the actual gambling he did in the casinos of Europe.

As if the world wasn't scary enough in Churchill's time, he would speak of the sense that he was sinking into the abyss . . . because financially he was. He would once draw himself as an overloaded little pig, carrying a twenty-thousand-pound weight on his back. Even during the Blitz, he was arguing with his agent over royalties and thinking about tax exemptions.

Why? *Why?* It was ill-discipline. It was an attempt to treat himself in a way his parents hadn't, to buy the love and fun he had missed out on. It was an attempt to prove himself, to keep up with the best and the brightest and richest of his time. Thankfully, Churchill was a vital and energetic man, but how much of this vitality was wasted? For what? And even if he was lucky enough to skate by, his son, who inherited his habits but not his talents, was not nearly so lucky. If only his father could have *held, held, held off.*

When your choices turn you into someone who has to worry about money, then you are not rich . . . no matter how much you make.

Across the Atlantic, the author F. Scott Fitzgerald wore himself out in similar fashion. He was infatuated with wealth, with glamor. He was driven and ungodly talented, but also impossibly immature and in a marriage that brought out the worst in both parties. "I used to write for myself," he lamented while staring at his mountainous debts. Now he wrote to keep the collectors at bay, to dig himself out of a hole with his editors or his friends. It destroyed his confidence . . . stole from him the love he had for his craft. Despite lifetime earnings of what would be *millions* today, he would die essentially broke, in a hotel room, alone. His fortune was gone and it had come at the cost of so many lost years of great writing.

"That poor son of a bitch," Dorothy Parker said as she looked down at a forty-four-year-old Fitzgerald in his casket. What struck her most was his worn and wrinkled hands, quietly evincing the toll of all the excess, all the indulgences, something not even the most skilled embalmer could hide.

If you have money, spend it . . . the problem is when people spend what they don't have, to get things they don't need, at a price nowhere near worth the cost.

Luckily, Churchill had just enough self-control—or perhaps good luck—that he never went fully over the edge. He never found the bottom of that abyss. But it was a close call. And how different the fate of the free world might have gone if he had . . .

What makes you think you can afford that risk? That you're so talented the spigot will never turn off? That you can burn the candle at both ends? That you won't be corrupted by your endless need for more, more, more?

It's worth taking a minute to clarify that living beyond one's means isn't the only form of reckless money management. The virtue of Cato's restraint can just as easily be taken to excess, as it perhaps even was by Cato. It's also irresponsible to be pennywise and pound foolish, to grind your life and vitality into dust trying to save miniscule amounts of money on things that don't matter.

Discipline with money is relative. The internet abounds with legitimately wealthy people sharing tips on how to reuse their trash bags or stack coupons to reduce the costs of things they should not even be thinking twice about.* They're not sweating the small stuff, they're sweating the *microscopic*. It's important to save, sure; we just want to make sure that this isn't costing us our most precious resource: *time*. It may well also cost us relationships with lovely people—our spouse, our children, our friends—who are not quite so strict with themselves.

For centuries, people on both extremes of the money spectrum have fundamentally misunderstood its value, its purpose. Fitzgerald thought that the rich were special, that they were different from other people. Hemingway would write in response, "Yes, they have more money."

Money isn't good or bad. It is a tool. Churchill's writing, for instance, supported him when he was exiled in the political wilderness. If money provides freedom or leverage, then great. If it

---

*We must be on guard against how easily this becomes greed, seeing money as all *ours*. Frugality and generosity rarely seem to go together.

becomes an addiction or a disorder—or worse, a distraction—not so great. Like any powerful tools, money also has its dangers and must be wielded safely and consciously (and is not for the weak-minded).

Money doesn't buy happiness . . . but it can buy you out of some frustrations. Nor can it give you freedom, if you are dependent on it to provide you with things you don't need . . . or more than any reasonable person actually needs.

The problem is that many of us tell ourselves that someday we'll be beyond this, that if we can just earn enough, be successful enough, we won't have to consider any of it. We will be beyond moderation and financial conscientiousness. We will have transcended the everyday worries of the common man. We can just do what we want, when we want, as much as we want. Because we'll be "good," we'll have "arrived."

Here's the thing: *This never happens.*

"Fuck-you money" is a chimera. You never get it. Nobody does. Poor people have poor-people problems and rich people have rich-people problems because people always have problems. You're always going to be subject to the necessity of self-discipline. Or at least, you'll never be immune from the consequence of ignoring it.

And is "fuck-you money" really such an admirable goal anyway? To have so much money you don't have to care about anyone or anything? That's not virtue, it's childishness. All you really need is enough money to be comfortable enough to politely say, "No, thanks. I'd rather not." To never have to do anything for a buck that's contrary to your values. To be able to stick with your main thing.

No amount of money is ever going to truly free you. But being less dependent, caring less about money? That will free you right now.

There's a quip from the Stoic Musonius Rufus who, dealing with a particularly frustrating person's greed, paid him quite a bit of money to go away. When a follower objected and pointed out the man's many faults, Musonius simply smiled and said, "Money is exactly what he deserves."

But this can cut both ways.

Plenty of people have made plenty . . . it doesn't have to make them worse. Lou Gehrig and Babe Ruth were both in the .001 percent. Queen Elizabeth and King George IV inherited the same priceless jewels and fortune. We decide which direction we'll go. Better or worse? A luxury or a burden?

We decide whether we'll *deserve* what we've gotten.

Get Better Every Day

~

Socrates didn't know much. There wasn't much he held for certain.

But he was sure, he said, that "we cannot remain as we are."

It doesn't matter who you are. It doesn't matter what you've done.

Nobody is as good as they could be. Nobody is perfect.

Everybody can improve.

There are few self-fulfilling prophecies more important or more dangerous than this.

If you think you have room to grow, you do and you will. If you think you're as good as you can be . . . you're right. You won't get any better.

It has been said that Tom Brady, the greatest quarterback in history—the youngest and the oldest to win a Super Bowl— isn't obsessed with winning. That's not what he focuses on. He's obsessed with improving the accuracy of his touchdown passes in the fourth quarter. He's obsessed with getting a little bit faster at releasing the football. He's not willing to stay the same, even though that "same" is very consistently the best in the league. The process of getting better, that's his drug. That's the dragon he chases, that's how he is able to defy aging and all expectations.

The Japanese word for this is *kaizen*. Continual improvement. Always finding something to work on, to make a little progress on. Never being satisfied, always looking to grow.

Revolution? Transformation? That's what amateurs chase. The pros are after *evolution*.

If the first step is just showing up, committing to doing something each day, then the next step is finding something to focus on getting *better at* each day. And in this, where cumulative improvement meets compounding returns we can harness one of the most powerful forces on Earth.

Think about it: Most people don't even show up. Of the people who do, most don't really push themselves. So to show up *and* be disciplined about daily improvement? You are the rarest of the rare.

And if improvement sounds difficult, how about just making fewer mistakes?

This is what Gehrig's manager said about him. The secret to Gehrig's incredible trajectory as an athlete wasn't just his commitment, it was that he never made the same mistake twice. The guy who began his career blowing at least one play per inning, improved to one mistake per game, to one per week, to one per month . . .

To err is human . . . but to err less each day is to become closer to the divine.

We not only hold ourselves to a standard, but we ratchet the standard up as we go; just as with weight training, what we're lifting should be steadily increasing with each subsequent workout. Our unwillingness to be satisfied with our performance, to be done with our progress, is what keeps us from plateauing. It drives us forward.

Is it a little discouraging that we never seem to "arrive"? That our standards rise just out of reach of our abilities? Absolutely not! We move the goalposts so the game doesn't get boring and, more important, so it never ends. Ultimately, this brings us more pleasure and more satisfaction. We reach heights we'd never have been able to see otherwise.

Do you want to be rotting or ripening? Are you getting better? Because if you're not . . . then you're probably getting worse.

Anyone, whether they're a professional athlete or a house-cleaner, can get better at their job. You can get better at being a person, a citizen, a son or a daughter. You can get better at how you think, how you focus, what you think about.

"Just as one person delights in improving his farm, and another his horse," Epictetus would say, riffing, as it happens, on Socrates, "so I delight in attending to my improvement day by day." He said this as a man who clawed his way out of slavery. He said this from exile. He said this as one of the wisest men in the ancient world. And still, he was focused on how he could get better every day, in every way.

One can imagine that, for Epictetus, this discipline would have been extremely helpful in those dark times. Because it gave him something to focus on—something only he controlled, not his master, not society, not his station in life. But this discipline is also helpful in the good times, too, preventing one from getting too cocky or complacent.

It doesn't matter what the scoreboard says, or the bank balance or the sales figures or the headlines. *You know.* You know whether you're getting better or worse, whether you're making progress day to day. And if you are? Wonderful. If you know there is room for improvement? Also wonderful. Either way, your marching orders are the same.

Come what may, success or failure, fame or misfortune, a focus on progress lets us look ourselves in the mirror with pride and ignore all the commotion in the background.

It's the journey of a lifetime. In fact, that's the way to think about all of this: How much progress could you make if you made just a little each day over the course of an entire life? What might this journey look like, where might it lead, if each bit of progress you made presented both the opportunity and the obligation to make a little more progress, and you seized those opportunities, you lived up to those obligations, each and every time?

Will you choose to take this journey? Will you continue on

even when you've reached further than you ever thought you could go? Or will you stop there?

Are you going to keep practicing? Or have you decided that this is *good enough*? That *you're* good enough?

Will you remain as you are? Or become what you're capable of?

Because once you stop getting better, there's only one direction to go . . .

"Do the best you can," the emperor says in Marguerite Yourcenar's beautiful novel *Memoirs of Hadrian.* "Do it over again. Then still improve, even if ever so slightly those retouches."

It's a beautiful irony: You're never content with your progress and yet, you're always content . . . because you're making progress.

Share the Load

~

In 1956, Harry Belafonte placed a call to Coretta Scott King. With her husband arrested once again, he was checking on her and whether the movement might need anything. But the two of them could barely carry on a conversation, because Coretta was continually getting pulled away from the phone to attend to one of the children, to take dinner out of the oven, to answer the door.

Sensing she was doing all of this alone, Belafonte politely asked why the Kings did not have any help at home. Well, she told him, Martin simply would not permit it. Such a luxury was a stretch on a minister's salary. They were worried people might judge them. It felt wrong for the Kings to so indulge themselves, while millions of black people suffered.

"That is absolutely ridiculous," Belafonte replied. "He's here in the middle of this movement doing all of these things, and he's going to get caught up in what people are going to think if he has somebody helping you?" *Your life is going to change right now*, Belafonte told her. He would personally pay for staff—and Martin had absolutely no say in the matter.

This wasn't just a nice gesture to an overworked family. It was also a strategic move. What Belafonte was buying Martin and Coretta was not just help, it was time. It was peace of mind. It was protection. He knew that with help, they would have more energy, more focus for the cause. They'd be stronger and more effective. The last thing he wanted Martin Luther King Jr. to worry about as he marched for peace and justice was whether there was milk in the fridge.

It takes discipline not to insist on doing everything yourself. Especially when you know how to do many of those things well. Especially when you have high standards about how they should be done. Even if you enjoy doing them—whether that's mowing your own lawn, writing your speeches, making your own schedule, or answering your own phone.

As Plutarch reminds us, while a leader must know how to do anything, they cannot conceivably do *everything*. It's not physically possible. It's not mentally possible.

Often, the best way to manage the load is to *share* the load.

Woe is the person who wears themselves out on trivial matters and then, when the big moments come, is out of energy. Woe is the person (and the people around them) who is so mentally exhausted and strung out because they've taken everything upon themselves that now, when things go wrong, there's no slack or cushion to absorb the additional stress.

A glutton isn't just someone who eats or drinks too much. Some of us are also gluttons for punishment. Gluttons for attention. Gluttons for control. Gluttons for work. What makes this so tricky to identify, let alone to manage, is that it often comes from a good place, as it did for Martin Luther King Jr. We feel obligated. We feel bad spending money. We feel guilty asking for help. No matter how well-intentioned, the outcome is the same: We wear ourselves down. We harm ourselves, we harm the cause, we neglect the main thing. We end up depriving the world of progress—of the benefits of what economists call the *law of comparative advantage.*

You have to be able to pass the ball . . . especially when somebody is open and has a better shot. You have to be able to share the minutes with other players, as those Spurs starters were willing to do, because that's what *teams* do.

The insecure are unable to do this. They fear being criticized. They fear letting people see behind the scenes. Tyrants are unable to do this. Egotists are unable to do this too. The cheap are unable to do this. They want it all for themselves. They aren't strong enough to bear being anything but the center, the exclusive, the sole source of achievement.

And what happens to most tyrannical regimes? They fail.

It doesn't make sense to try to do everything yourself. You have to delegate. You have to find people who are good at things and empower them to help you. You have to be strong enough to hand over the keys, to relinquish control, to develop a system—an organization—that is bigger than just us. If you want to keep the main thing the main thing, maybe you need to hire someone who can be a buffer for you—someone who says "No" for you.

Our willpower is not enough. We shouldn't have to just gut it out. We need to share. That is, if you're trying to *scale.* Trying to build or do something that matters, something bigger than just you.

There is a certain amount of privilege in this, sure. Not all of us can afford to hire full-time staff or have a patron willing to pick up the tab. But each of us must know what an hour of our time is worth. We must have the discipline to figure out how best to spend that time and how to invest the fruit it bears.

No matter how successful or important you are, we all have tasks that can be automated. We all have legacy tasks that ought to be reassigned. Everything in life is a team sport.

You know these inefficiencies exist, and yet you refuse to delegate them. You continue to try to do everyone's job.

Stop procrastinating. Delegate!

This will not be cheap, and it would be ignorant and arrogant to insist otherwise, but the value is virtually incalculable, because it affords you the most expensive thing in the world: time.

By compelling Martin Luther King Jr. to delegate, Belafonte was giving the man—and by extension, society—more time to do his essential work. Figuratively, we all face a ticking clock, but King's was tragically shorter. Every minute that he and Coretta didn't have to spend on chores at home was time well spent.

But also what of the time they got to spend together? Because delegation doesn't just provide time but also space—freedom. It allows us to brief, to think, to connect, to appreciate. King was later asked by an interviewer what he would do with an uninterrupted week of rest. After scoffing at the pure impossibility of such a thing, given the injustices of the world and the demands of the Civil Rights Movement at the time, King explained what he would do:

> If I had the luxury of an entire week, I would spend it meditating and reading, refreshing myself spiritually and intellectually. . . . Amidst the struggle, amidst the frustrations, amidst the endless work, I often reflect that I am forever *giving*—never pausing to take in. I feel urgently the need for even an hour of time to get away, to withdraw, to refuel. I need more time to think through what is being done, to take time out from the mechanics of the movement, to reflect on the *meaning* of the movement.

What would you manage to do with a week like this? With an hour? With a little help that would allow you to carve out some extra time and space for yourself? But not just any kind of time. Time to reflect and to think. And not just any kind of space. Space to learn, space to plan.

Together, that little bit of time and space each day combine to form an opportunity to meditate on what is important to us and to examine how we're doing in life.

You deserve that. But there's only one way you'll get it.

It's by delegating. It's by asking for help. It's by making a change.

Respect Time

~

As a rookie for the New York Knicks, a young Phil Jackson mostly rode the bench. One night, toward the end of a game, Jackson was in the middle of a conversation with another backup when the coach, Red Holzman, caught him by surprise. "How much time is left, Jackson?" he demanded. "One minute and twenty-eight seconds," he answered. *No, how much time is on the shot clock?* Red replied and of course, Jackson didn't know. "Well, you've got to know," the disgusted coach told him. "You may be going into the game, and if you don't know the time, you could get us in trouble. Don't let me catch you doing that again."

We are all given the same twenty-four hours each day, just as each basketball team is given twenty-four seconds per possession on the court. To not be aware of it? To not respect it? To not know how to use and manage it? It is not just sloppy, it's stupid.

You're in the game, always. You've got to know the time precisely because you will never know when it's going to run out on you. That's what the reminder *memento mori* means. No one can take time or life for granted . . . as it runs out for all of us.

The pursuit of discipline means being disciplined in all things, especially little things. And time—how we spend it, its tiny increments—is something small that actually amounts to something very large.

Some people claim that time is just a construct. If that is true, it is perhaps humanity's greatest creation. Because time is the way we measure the only truly nonrenewable resource we have. No one is making more of it. Once lost, it cannot be recovered. It is also an incredibly powerful force, as anyone who has ever watched small amounts of interest applied over a long enough period can attest.

You see, time that is wasted is also wasting us. When we kill time, we are killing ourselves. We have to learn how to use time or else it will use us . . . up.

That is why we do our work promptly. Why we get to the point. Why we stick to the agenda. Why we don't drone on, don't tolerate digressions or indulge distractions. It's why we keep our desk clean—so we don't waste time looking for stuff. It's why we get up early—so we have *more* time, uninterrupted time, at the freshest part of the day. It's why we're deliberate about what we say yes and no to, because we understand that time is a gift—and what we give it to matters.

More practically, the poet W. H. Auden said that "The modern stoic knows that the surest way to discipline passion is to discipline time: decide what you want or ought to do during the day, then always do it exactly the same moment every day, and passion will give you no trouble." Now, one doesn't have to follow this advice literally to still see the deeper message: Routine is an essential tool in the management of time and the suppression of those negative forces of distraction, procrastination, and laziness.

The person who wakes up *whenever,* wakes up and does *whatever,* orders their day *however*? This is a person who will never have enough time, who will always be behind. But the more disciplined person, the Toni Morrison, who gets up when they ought to; the person like William Stafford, who tackles the hard projects first; who, like Booker T. Washington, says no to what is not essential? This is a person who makes full use of their time.

Take a minute to think about how you spent the last year, the last month, the last week, the last day. Think about how much of it was wasted, how much of it was half-assed, how much of it was spent in reaction to things out of your control. And even if you have decent results to show for this time, still, you could have done better. We all could have.

The moments between the moments we let pass us by, the things we did lazily and had to do again, the things we agreed to that we shouldn't have. We could have done all those things better . . . except we can't. There is simply no escaping the fact that those moments are gone forever, that you will *never get that time back.*

You missed opportunities to get better. You missed opportunities to make progress. You didn't let patience work to your advantage. You disrespected other people (who you made wait). You disrespected your cause (which you deprived of your presence).

But the silver lining of this tragedy is that life has given you a second chance.

At least for now. Because you have today. You have the present moment.

How will you spend it? What will you make of it? What will it amount to?

And let's be clear, that doesn't just mean hurrying along. Queen Elizabeth's mother was once rushed along at a public by an aide who claimed they were out of time. "Time is not my dictator," the Queen Mother said as she stopped and shook hands with each person who had waited to see her. "I dictate to time."

While time *is* ultimately the dictator of our presence here on this earth, we *do* dictate how we spend it. As long as we are aware of it, aware of its value and the importance of managing it well. As long as we are putting it to work for us, even as it is working against us in the mortal sense.

Now is the time. Because *now* is the only time you have.

Put Up Boundaries

~

George Washington was famous for his reserve, keeping his emotions and personal feelings to himself. Angela Merkel's closest aides have never seen inside her apartment.

It's remarkable to think that after an entire lifetime in front of the cameras for Queen Elizabeth, after meeting so many people, after so many appearances and speeches and audiences with world leaders, almost no one can answer that tantalizing, fascinating question:

"What is the Queen like?"

Imagine, she has never once spoken on the record to a reporter . . . in seven decades! The Shah of Iran once asked her if, over her reign, she'd had more Labour or Conservative prime ministers. As it happened, the Queen didn't know—because it wasn't her business. It wouldn't have been appropriate.

Elizabeth is not just an observer of the various rules of her profession; her restraint goes further than just not getting involved in politics. Her grandchildren attest that she rarely gives them explicit advice and *never* tells them what they must do.

Instead, she finds that the right question, or better, just a non-judgmental ear, allows them to figure it out for themselves.

All this in a word?

Boundaries.

And sadly, this kind of discipline is all too rare these days.

In a world of social media, instant gratification, and the celebration of shamelessness, we don't much respect people who establish and maintain boundaries. You know, minding your own business. Setting the rules of engagement. Keeping your private life private. Not letting people drag you down into the muck. Not getting entangled in other people's dysfunctions (or entangling them in yours). Being strong enough to communicate what you like and dislike. Respecting other people's space and preferences.

This is seemingly basic stuff that basically nobody has a handle on.

Think of all the words we have to describe people like this:

Oversharers
Hot messes
Doormats
Drama queens
Busybodies
Pushovers
Shit stirrers
Gossipmongers

We live in a time of vulgarity and silliness and immaturity and selfishness. A time of freedom that we have decided is actually license for stupidity, unseriousness, and excess. Look at our heroes: Reality TV stars. Influencers. Professional wrestlers. YouTubers. Demagogues.

These are not heroes. These are cautionary tales. The people we ought to admire are quiet. Dignified. Reserved. Serious. Professional. Respectful of themselves and others.

Plutarch reminded leaders that they were unlikely to warrant much in the way of worship from their subjects if they were too often seen around the fire, munching on beans. He was talking about the kind of distance and reserve that Queen Elizabeth and Angela Merkel and George Washington all practiced. Cato for his part was an avid defender of what was known as the *mos maiorum*. You know, the unspoken and yet also spoken way of life of your grandparents. Those rules, somewhere between manners and morals, that tell us how to act, how to treat people, how to carry ourselves, what to do when you get a speeding ticket, or what to do when there is space between what we can get away with and what the laws or rules say.

But it's about more than just that.

Boundaries are about drawing some lines around yourself— healthy borders between what you'll share and what you won't, what you'll accept and what you won't, how you treat others and how you expect to be treated, what is your responsibility and what isn't. Or as Jay-Z explained once, particularly in regard to adjusting to his success and fame, "It's about knowing who you are, and just doing what's comfortable for you, and not letting people pull you in a thousand different directions. Because if you allow [it] . . . people will have you doing all kinds of stuff, but it has to make sense for *you*."

Keeping the main thing the main thing is impossible if you're not capable of saying no or pushing back when others put too much on your plate. You can't keep your head about you in stressful situations if you have no idea who you are or what you stand for. You can't be a strong parent if you're a mess or if you're still letting your parents walk all over you. How will you get anything done if the temptations of social media rule your life? How can you get back up after a failure if you are overly concerned with what other people think of you? You won't do your best work if you're constantly micromanaging everyone else's.

There is a term—*energy vampires*—meant to describe the kind of people who, because of their lack of boundaries, suck others dry with their neediness, their selfishness, their dysfunction, and their drama. Not only must you not be an energy vampire yourself, but you must be aware that these type of people exist. You must be strong enough to keep them at arm's distance— even if they're beautiful, even if they're talented, even if they're family or old friends from childhood, even if their helplessness calls to the most empathetic part of yourself.

A country without borders, it has been said, is not really a country at all. So it goes with people. Without boundaries, we are overwhelmed. We are stretched too thin. So thin that those features that previously defined us start to disappear until there's no telling where we start and the energy vampires around us end.

This is why we clean up our desk. This is why we ignore provocations that have nothing to do with us. This is why we don't speak every thought that pops into our head, why we have to figure out how to be responsible with our finances and manage our time efficiently. Why we go to bed on time, every time, and wake up early every morning.

Because we are trying to corral our lives, our emotions, our concerns in such a way that it's possible to manage them all. That we are controlling them instead of the other way around.

Understand: Most of the people doing important work are people you've never heard of—they want it that way. Most happy people don't need you to know how happy they are—they aren't thinking about you at all. *Everyone* is going through something, but some people choose not to vomit their issues on everyone else. The strongest people are self-contained. They keep themselves in check. They keep their business where it belongs . . . their business.

Is it true that some people will get away with conduct unbecoming of an [insert]? Yes. They may even have fun or get rich doing it. And? Our boundaries leave that concern to them. We know that in the end they are punishing themselves.

As William Penn famously said, those with strong boundaries "are so much more their own that, paying common dues, they are rulers of all the rest."

Set your boundaries. Enforce them—gently but firmly. Treat everyone else's with as much respect as you'd want for your own.

Be the adult in a world of emotional children.

Do Your Best

~

A promising young officer named Jimmy Carter was applying for a spot in the Navy's nuclear submarine program. There he sat, for more than two hours, across from Admiral Hyman Rickover, who not only created the world's first nuclear Navy through sheer willpower in 1955, but he ran it with an intense focus for the next three decades, which included interviewing, in person, every single person who would touch his prized submarines.

As they sat and talked, they covered a wide range of topics from current events to naval tactics, electronics, and physics. Carter had prepared for weeks for the interview and sweated through each question, as Rickover—never smiling—steadily ratcheted up the difficulty. Then finally, he lobbed what seemed like a softball: "How did you stand in your class in the Naval Academy?"

"Sir, I stood fifty-ninth in a class of 820," Carter said, swelling with pride. But having, seen, by then, generations of America's best military talent, Rickover was not particularly impressed by rank. "But did you do your best?" he asked the young man.

Of course, Carter felt himself rushing to answer, as we all might if asked such a question. But before he could, something inside stopped short. What about the times he had been tired? What about the classes when he'd been confident enough in his grades that he could coast? What about the questions he hadn't asked or the times he'd been distracted? What about the professors he'd found boring and paid little attention to? What about the extra reading he could have done—on weapons systems, on history, on science, on trigonometry? What about the morning PT he'd shuffled through?

"No, sir," he found himself confessing, "I didn't *always* do my best."

And with this, Rickover, got up to leave, asking one final question, before he departed:

"Why not?"

Why didn't you do your best? It was a question that would take many shapes, and challenge and inspire the young man in many ways for the rest of his life.

As in:

Why are you holding back?

Why are you half-assing this?

Why are you so afraid to try?

Why don't you think this matters?

What could you be capable of if you really committed?

If you're not giving your best, *why are you doing it at all?*

You might think from this exchange that Rickover was a ruthless taskmaster who refused to accept excuses for failure. This is partly correct. His exacting standards—which he expected of himself and anyone he hired—not only transformed the United States into a global power, but it also propelled Carter, eventually, into the presidency.

Still, in his single term, Carter's successes—no foreign wars, a peace settlement between Israel and Egypt, negotiating and ratifying the Panama Canal Treaties, normalizing diplomatic relations with the People's Republic of China—were also accompanied by struggles. One such area was in energy policy, where, in a 1977 address to the nation, a forward-thinking Carter declared energy and climate change the "moral equivalent to war." Although he knew his proposals were going to be unpopular among the American people, he said, "It was impossible for me to imagine the bloody legislative battles ahead." He'd fight the war against Congress for his entire term and was mocked for putting solar panels on the White House. Despite his efforts and his sincerity, Carter fell short.

Rickover, the ruthless taskmaster, nonetheless beamed with pride.

"There is no question that the public will ultimately understand and he will be regarded as a far-seeing man who has attempted to protect the people of the US," he said of Carter's energy efforts. "It took about four hundred years for the Lord

Jesus Christ to have his message accepted. Up to that time he would be considered a 'failure.' As long as a man is trying as hard as he can to do what he thinks to be right, he is a success, regardless of the outcome."

This is the wonderful thing about doing your best. It insulates you, ever so slightly, from outcomes as well as ego. It's not that you don't care about results. It's that you have a kind of trump card. Your success doesn't go to your head because you know you're capable of more. Your failures don't destroy you because you are sure there wasn't anything more *you* could have done.

You always control whether you give your best or not. No one can stop you from that.

You don't have to end up number one in your class. Or win everything, every time. In fact, not winning is not particularly important.

What does matter is that you gave everything, because anything less is to cheat the gift.

The gift of your potential.

The gift of the opportunity.

The gift of the craft you've been introduced to.

The gift of the responsibility entrusted to you.

The gift of the instruction and time of others.

The gift of life itself.

Ralph Ellison was a student at the Tuskegee Institute when his piano teacher Hazel Harrison gave him the gift not just of her time and energy but also a way of thinking about the obligation that every performer and talented person has. "You must *always* play your best," she had told him, "even if it's only in the waiting room at Chehaw Station, because in this country there'll always be a little man hidden behind the stove . . . [who knows] the *music* and the tradition, and the standards of musicianship required for whatever you've set out to perform."

Chehaw Station was the train station outside the campus. The little man behind the stove? That became the artistic conscience that guided Ellison, much like the Rickover's standards hovered over Carter, just like the dictum of John Wooden guided his players from the day of his first lesson in the basics of putting on a pair of socks:

"Your best is good enough."

Not perfect. Your *best*.

Leave the rest to the scoreboard, to the judges, to the gods, to fate, to the critics.

Beyond the Temperament . . .

Rarely does a person who competes with his head as well
as his body come out second.

PETE CARRIL

It would be wonderful if being smart or brilliant, successful or
powerful, was a free pass. It emphatically is not.

In fact, we find that because of our talents, because of our
resources, because of our responsibilities, we have to be *more* in
command of ourselves. We have to consciously, considerately,
constantly check in, check ourselves, check our impulses.

We must follow that old dictum to *know thyself* physically
and mentally. And to follow it with a second and equally ancient
dictum, *nothing in excess.*

We work hard, we think hard, we hold hard to high standards. If we do this consistently, we will be happy and productive. And in those rare instances when we fail, which we will, we

will be all right. Not only because we'll know, in our hearts, that we did our best, but because we have the strength and character to *endure* setbacks on our journey. We'll have the determination and the balance to get back up and keep going.

If we don't? If we fall into excess, if we lapse on our standards, what then? If we are careless and lazy, sloppy and weak, if we stop attending to our improvement, the great Epictetus tells us we will stop making progress and we will live and die as ordinary, disappointing people.

But it is more than that. Speaking of Alcibiades, the once promising and committed student of Socrates, Plutarch illustrated the costs of intemperance not just to ourselves but also to the people who depend on us.

> . . . his lack of discipline and the audacity of his way of life destroyed him and he deprived the city of all his benefits on account of his extravagance and licentiousness.

Self-discipline is not just our destiny, it is our *obligation*.

To our potential.

To our country.

To our cause.

To our families.

To our fellow human beings.

To those who look up to us.

To those who come after us.

Because soon enough you will be truly tested—beyond the ordinary ways in which you have had to persist and resist on this journey toward your best self. Life will demand something greater, something bordering on heroic.

Your body, your mind, your spirit will have to align so that you might discover that you are capable of more than you thought possible. You will also be asked to give . . . more than you have ever had to give (or give up) before.

PART III

THE MAGISTERIAL
(THE SOUL)

When we rule ourselves, we have the responsibilities of
sovereigns, not of subjects.

THEODORE ROOSEVELT

It's not uncommon to find someone who has physical command of themselves. Nor is there a shortage of brilliant people
who have brought their mind and spirit under control in the
pursuit of this profession or that one. What is extraordinarily
rare is someone who not only combines these two disciplines,
and manages to do so in the so-called arena—in public life, as a
doer, a contributor to society. Of course, temperance and restraint can be found in the monasteries and the mountain retreat; that's not what we're after. Can you achieve this stillness,
this balance, in the chaos of real life? Surrounded by temptation? Whether the crowd cheers or jeers? Regardless of what

would be tolerated, what you could get away with, what people even think is possible? We call this rare and transcendent plane the Magisterial—mastering yourself, mentally, physically, in command always, in all forms . . . and somehow finding a gear beyond that, finding more to give, more to draw from yourself. This is the greatness we seek, this is where the body, the mind, and the spirit come together in life's most stressful situations, when things don't go our way, in moments of destiny or great difficulty, where we show what all these sacrifices were for, where we show what we were made of, where we prove that is in fact possible to possess the world *and* keep our soul.

Elevating Yourself . . .

~

For twenty-five years, Antoninus fought his way to the top of Roman politics and now, finally, the Emperor Hadrian, in the throes of a protracted, mortal illness, was ready to give him what he had earned: the crown.

"I have found you an Emperor, noble, mild, obedient, sensible, neither headstrong and nurse through youth nor careless through old age—Antoninus Aurelius," Hadrian said of this universally beloved leader.

Except it was a cruel trick.

Though Antoninus's faultless service as quaestor, praetor, consul, and Senator, his flawless character and impeccable record had prepared him for power in a way few ever had been, Hadrian and fate had other plans. Despite his kind words about Antoninus, Hadrian believed that the true future of Rome lay in someone else, specifically, a boy named Marcus. Antoninus would be his placeholder—a preposterously overqualified throne-warmer.

The true history of sovereigns is nothing like the symbolic and grandmotherly reign of the modern Queen Elizabeth. The ancient world was a brutal, violent place. Surely, once at the top, Antoninus would consolidate power, protect himself, and ensure a legacy that would stand for all time. He would *prove* that he had been underestimated. He would *take* what his ambition craved.

Except, again, no.

Despite it all, over a reign of some twenty-three years and the impossible, unenviable job of preparing a boy to replace him, Antoninus managed a master class in temperance. He was not just a balanced and decent human, but was balanced and decent as the head of an enormous empire whose millions of subjects literally worshipped him as an all-powerful god-king!

Never once did he put himself first. Never once did he prefer his own family's interests. Instead of complaining or scheming, he quietly got to work on what must have seemed, at least at first, to be a completely unfair, totally thankless job. Not once in his reign, the ancient historians would remark, was Antoninus responsible for the shedding of a single drop of blood, foreign or domestic. This gentleness and devotion to his country, to their cause, to those he loved would earn him a cognomen that, while not as glorious as Alexander the Great or as awesome as William the Conqueror, is all the more magnificent: Antoninus *Pius*.

Temperance, when pursued with this level of dedication, done amid the kind of temptation and stress that Antoninus Pius faced, as the head of an empire comprised of some seventy or eighty million people and some 3.5 million square miles, was a holy thing.

Everything that Queen Elizabeth is in ceremony, the Roman emperor was in fact. The emperor had the power to pass laws and enforce them, sitting in review of legal cases. He had the power to wage war and sat at the head of the world's most ruthless war machine. He had the power to add or remove days from the week, having complete control over the Roman calendar. He had the power to write and, being *pontifex maximus*, the chief of religious affairs, rewrite the dogma of Roman religion.

We know what most emperors did with this power. Pages, volumes, *libraries*, have been filled with their misdeeds and excesses.

So why, then, as the exception to the Roman rule, is Antoninus not so well-known?

Such is the irony of temperance. It makes us greater *and* much less likely to crave recognition for that greatness. Not only was Antoninus notoriously indifferent to superficial honors, he actively avoided them. In a gesture of love toward the end of his reign, the Senate offered to rename the months of September and October after Antoninus and his wife, which he promptly declined. July and August remain named after Julius Caesar and Augustus Caesar some two thousand years later. Antoninus, for his humility, received no such eternal fame.

If anything, Antoninus became a *victim* of his success. According to the nineteenth-century historian Ernest Renan,

"Antoninus would have had the reputation of being the best of sovereigns if he had not designated for his successor a man equal to himself in goodness and in modesty—one who joined to these shining qualities talent, and a charm which make an image to live in the recollection of mankind." By not assassinating his rival, by instead committing fully to shaping his replacement, Marcus Aurelius, into a great man—a man whose fame eventually outshone the adopted father who had cultivated it— Antoninus condemned himself to the footnotes of history.

At the root of the word *discipline* is the Latin *discipulus,* or pupil. It implies the existence of a student but also a teacher. This is the beauty of the relationship between Antoninus and Marcus Aurelius. One man, who, despite his self-interest, had the self-control and the kindness to be a tutor and mentor. The other was willing to learn, humble enough to be the *disciple* of a teacher of such self-discipline and goodness that after his death, he would be deified.

Each of them responded to the unusual circumstances that brought them together, which neither of them chose and nearly all of history would have predicted would end in disaster, and together they reached a kind of greatness that stretches beyond the imagination. The kind that belongs in storybooks and parables, not that decorates the cruel halls of power.

What exactly did Antoninus teach Marcus?

Let's start with the body.

There was a real toughness to Antoninus. He impressed the

young man in the way he could "have one of his migraines and then go right back to what he was doing—fresh and at the top of his game." Antoninus took good care of himself, not just because health is important, but because in health he could better conduct the business of the empire. "Not a hypochondriac or obsessed with his appearance," Marcus wrote of his father's health-consciousness, "but not ignoring things either. With the result that he hardly ever needed medical attention, or drugs or any sort of salve or ointment." Antoninus showed Marcus that it was perfectly possible for a man of great power and wealth to live without a troop of bodyguards or the charades and pretensions of his position. Marcus observed his adopted father as he behaved in almost every way as an ordinary person yet never appearing "slovenly or careless as a ruler or when carrying out official obligations."

If the task needed to be done, Antoninus did it with energy, straight through from dawn to dusk most days. It was a minor thing, but Marcus even noted the way that Antoninus kept a simple diet, kept hydrated but scheduled his bathroom breaks so that he might not be called away from state business at inopportune moments. To Antoninus, these were not minor things, but symbolic, important things. We're told that as he got older and his back began to stoop, he took to putting thin pieces of lindenwood in his clothes to keep his posture straight. He was already ramrod straight, figuratively. He made sure that stayed literally true as well.

But we should not mistake this strictness for an unpleasant life.

On the contrary. "He had the ability both to refrain from and enjoy the things that most people are too weak to refrain from and too inclined to enjoy," Marcus said of Antoninus, likening his capacity for maintaining this difficult balance to Socrates, who was notably frugal but notoriously fun. He had "strength of will," Marcus wrote in *Meditations,* "the ability to persevere in the one situation and remain sober in the other." Life handed Antoninus material comforts in abundance, which he accepted and utilized without arrogance or dependence. "If they were there," Marcus noted, "he took advantage of them. If not, he didn't miss them."

As for temperament?

Once again, Antoninus was the model. He would teach Marcus "unwavering adherence to decisions, once he'd reached them," which meant never letting go of things "before he was sure he had examined them thoroughly, understood them perfectly." What was most striking about Antoninus was "his searching questions at meetings . . . a kind of single mindedness, almost, never content with first impressions, or breaking off the discussion prematurely." He knew "when to push and when to back off," how to walk that most precarious, delicate line. No matter what he was dealing with, an issue was to be "approached logically and with due consideration, in a calm and orderly fashion but decisively and with no loose ends." He stayed on topic and was not easily distracted. Though he would have been indulged in them, he didn't go on tangents or bore people with long stories. And when he messed up, Antoninus owned his mistakes—fearing neither responsibility nor blame.

No leader, no matter how good they are, can hope to avoid criticism. Antoninus received plenty of it, much of it unfair and unwarranted, but he declined to return pettiness with pettiness. He ignored informers and gossips. He tolerated being questioned because it made him better, even if it meant admitting error. Unlike Nero, who once exiled a poet for being talented, he took delight at seeing his ideas improved upon. Despite his brilliance and authority, Antoninus had no problem yielding the floor to experts and deferring to their advice—a skill few with unlimited power happen to have, fewer manage to keep, and fewer still bother to grow.

To see Antoninus get upset at work was a rare thing. It was rarer with friends. And nobody, according to Marcus, saw him sweat. Despite the stresses of the job, "he never exhibited rudeness, lost control of himself, or turned violent." If this seems like faint praise, it's worth noting that Hadrian once stabbed a secretary in the eye with a pen for making a mistake.

Flattery had no effect on Antoninus, yet he went out of his way to put others at ease. When he visited friends, he was able to put the pretentions of the office aside and be with them as an ordinary person, taking care not to be treated any differently than anyone else. One friend, ribbing Antoninus after the emperor made some observations about the decor, felt perfectly comfortable telling the man, who had power of life and death over all the empire's subjects, that "When you enter another man's home you should be deaf and dumb."

He could laugh and be laughed at. He took the job seriously but never himself. He was, to borrow Marcus's phrase, the perfect combination of a person who had "gravity without airs."

Although Hadrian had taken long state tours through the provinces of the empire, Antoninus declined. Having served as proconsul to Italia and then Asia prior to his ascension, he understood what an immense burden these trips were on the people who had to host the imperial processions. No matter how humbling and unassuming he tried to be, the baggage train of a sovereign was an imposition, and he tried not to impose it on anyone if it could be avoided.

It was this physical and mental discipline that converged in Antoninus to make him a compassionate, measured, and unwavering man who ruled himself first. Fate hadn't shaken out exactly as Antoninus may have hoped, but he managed to turn it into something that, in retrospect, he would have not traded for anything. For those twenty-three stable years, he ruled Rome, he bonded deeply with Marcus, and he watched Rome not only flourish but then pass into equally able and measured hands.

If fame was not to be his reward, he still earned the ultimate triumph for anyone in politics—ending his career with clean hands and, as Marcus Aurelius most admired, a clear conscience.

In AD 161, the end of Antoninus's time was upon him. Mustering "the calmness of an accomplished sage," it was said, he prepared to face death. Putting his final affairs in order, he transferred command to his adopted son, but not before uttering his final word—a piece of advice, an encapsulation of his existence, a goal for each of us—*Aequanimitas.*

Equanimity.

Now it was Marcus's turn to live up to the crown, to live up to the example Antoninus had set for him.

Equanimity would be the perfect watchword.

You look at the before and after pictures of American presidents and it's clear: Being head of state weighs on a person. Heavy is the head that wears the crown . . . and gray goes the hair underneath it. The enormous responsibility grinds a leader down steadily except in the moments when it overwhelms them. It would be easy to say, "The weak need not apply," but they often do—harming themselves and the people they're supposed to serve in the process.

Fate gifted Antoninus many years of peace and stability. Marcus Aurelius would not be so lucky. He would face historic flooding, a barbarian invasion, and a devastating plague that killed millions. A close friend would betray and try to kill him. The decline and fall of Rome was upon him . . . it wasn't his fault, but it was his responsibility. It was his daily nightmare.

Imagine the terror and the frustration and the sheer stress.

Lives were on the line. His own family was in danger. Nothing could possibly prepare a person for this much adversity. Every day another crisis, another problem stretching his already thin resources thinner. When fear and anger collided within previous emperors, Rome's streets ran red with blood.

Not with Marcus. He steadfastly dispatched dire situation after dire situation, not just refusing to compromise his principles but insisting on displaying them for all to see. He let the Roman people know, through dictum and deed, that his was not fair-weather temperance but marrow-deep self-control.

A normal person, a lesser (and, sad to say, more typical) leader might lament this parade of tragedies. Not Marcus. It wasn't *bad* that this stuff happened to him. It was an opportunity. "The impediment to action advances action," he wrote to himself, "*what stands in the way becomes the way*." All the adversity, all the difficulty—as well as the awful power and luxury—was an opportunity for him to prove himself. To show that he had really learned from Antoninus, that he didn't just believe in temperance, but that he lived it.

When Tiberius became emperor in AD 14, he installed himself in an island pleasure palace on Capri. Nero, free of his mother's influence, called for his lyre and styled himself Rome's most talented artist, ignoring state business to indulge his ego. Speaking of Tiberius and these cautionary tales, Marcus would observe how "trivial the things we want so passionately are. And how much more philosophical it would be to take what we've given and show uprightness, self-control, obedience to God, without making a production of it."

Which is precisely what he did . . . though not without some self-doubt first.

Marcus Aurelius reportedly wept when he was told he would become king—he knew his history, it was not a blessing that many emerged from better off. It would be a hard job—not just to be emperor, but to be a good one, to not be corrupted or destroyed by it.

There must have been moments when he wanted to do just about anything else, when he would have preferred his books and his philosophy to the burdens of what destiny had chosen for him. "Even if you attain the wisdom of Cleanthes or Zeno," one of his tutors wrote to him, "yet against your will you must put on the purple cloak, not the philosopher's woolen cape."

Could he do it? Could he wear it with honor and dignity, not be stained by it? Facing the possibility of breaking bad like Caligula, like Vespasian, like Claudius, he was sick to his stomach.

He would dream one night that his shoulders were made of ivory. *Yes,* he was strong enough. It *was* possible not to be destroyed by the job. He could do it. He *would* do it. He would *not* be like them. He would use the job as a canvas to paint a masterpiece.

It is said that no man is a hero to his valet, but Marcus, who was even closer to Antoninus than a valet, who had seen the man at his best and his worst for more than two decades, still worshipped him. His other tutors, his study of Stoicism, his advisors, would all play a part in Marcus's ultimate success, but as Renan wrote, "Superior to all these masters who had been selected from every corner of the globe, Marcus had a single master whom he revered above them all; and that was Antoninus, . . . It was because Marcus Aurelius had by his side the most beautiful model of a perfect life, and one whom he understood and loved, that he became what he was."

And Antoninus *was* a hero. He *earned* that worship, not in one brave moment on the battlefield, but through the extraordinary, ordinary discipline he demanded of himself day to day. Marcus, observing, witnessed it and was inspired by it, and committed his life to it.

That's the thing about discipline . . . like courage, it is contagious.

Marcus caught it from Antoninus and became who he was, what he was. Which is to say, incredible.

When Marcus was crowned, when the singular power that had belonged to Antoninus was given to him, he faced a test not unlike the one his beloved model had faced. Because through Hadrian's strange succession plan, Marcus had inherited a stepbrother whose role was uncertain. What should an emperor do with this potential rival?

An ancient Stoic master had warned a previous emperor to dispatch any other male heirs, saying one "cannot have too many Caesars." Marcus thought and thought and came upon a solution unmatched in all of history for its generosity and self-lessness, literally a walking contradiction of the dictum that absolute power corrupts absolutely: He named his stepbrother *co-emperor.* Given absolute power . . . the first thing he did was give half of it away.

Marcus Aurelius and his stepbrother could not have been more different either. Lucius Verus was not nearly so strict with himself. He was not known to have ever picked up a philosophy book. Did Marcus believe himself to be superior? From his *Meditations,* all we hear him express is gratitude "that I had the kind of brother I did. One whose character challenged me to improve my own. One whose love and affection enriched my life."

It was said that the true majesty of Marcus Aurelius was that his exactingness was directed only at himself. He did not "go around expecting Plato's Republic." People were people, he understood they were not perfect. He found a way to work with flawed people, putting them to service for the good of the empire, searching them for virtues that he celebrated and accepting their vices, which he knew were not in his control.

"We are so far from possessing anything of our own," Marcus said to the Senate of his family's so-called wealth, "that even the house in which we live is yours." One of the only direct commands we hear of him giving the Senate was that they be merciful to some of his political enemies who had attempted a coup.

The majority of Marcus Aurelius's commands were instead

to himself. Robin Waterfield, his translator, observes that 300 of the 488 entries in *Meditations* are rules Marcus gave himself. He got up early. He journaled. He kept himself active. He was not blessed with good health, but he never complained, never used it as an excuse, never let it slow him down more than absolutely necessary. Despite his wealth and power, he lived humbly— maintaining that difficult balance of restraint within abundance, spending most of his reign not in glamorous palaces of marble but in the simple tent of a soldier at the front.

And when he fell short or screwed up? He tried to pick himself up and get back to it. To do his best always, even when it was very hard.

In the depths of the Antonine Plague, as Rome's treasury was depleted, Marcus held a two-month sale on the lawn of the imperial palace, selling off his jewels and art collection, his wife's silks and everything else they could live without. Were there other ways he could have solved the empire's financial problems? Of course. He could have raised taxes. He could have looted the provinces. He could have relied on "prescription"—to seize the estates and property of Rome's oligarchs. He also could have just kicked the can down the road, leaving the issue to his successors. Nearly every emperor before and after him would take these easy ways out, never thinking twice about it.

Marcus took the hit instead.

Because that's what great leaders do: They do the right thing, even when—*especially when*—it costs them.

When he was criticized, he shrugged it off. He had no time for sycophants or slanderers. Like Antoninus, when he was shown to be incorrect, he admitted error and changed his mind. It was a busy, ceaseless life, but he found stillness inside it, managing even to study philosophy from the cot in his tent, far from his library. He worked hard to be present, to "concentrate every minute like a Roman," winnowing his thoughts and tuning out distraction, doing what was in front of him with both the tenderness and the tenacity he had learned from his hero. Whatever it was, he did his best—whether he was celebrated or despised for it.

"You don't have to turn this into something," he reminded himself when someone did something wrong or said something untrue about him. When he lusted after something, he stopped himself, turning those desires to stone before they burned through him and he did something he'd regret. He tried to make beautiful choices, tried to look for the best in people, tried to put himself in their shoes, tried to lead by serving. It was the pride of Marcus's life that he not only didn't need to ask anyone for favors but that anytime anyone asked him for something— money, advice, a hand—he could be generous.

Amid plenty, amid intrigue, Marcus kept and *was kept by,* this beautiful motto:

"Unrestrained moderation."

It is one thing to be a king, it is another to be a *philosopher-king,* and another thing entirely to be a *good philosopher-king.* To be a kingly *person*, independent of your title. Enfranchised, indifferent to what makes no difference, self-contained, self-motivated, devoted, hitting every right note at the right time in the right way. The kind of character that Marcus Aurelius cultivated was such that it brought distinction to his position, rather than the position bringing honor to his person.

To remain oneself in a world that pushes for conformity takes courage. It takes courage as well as temperance to be restrained in a world of excess, where we attack and mock those who don't indulge in the pleasures we have rationalized and the passions we have excused in ourselves.

Did he lose his temper from time to time? Of course. Few leaders can claim otherwise. But the ancient historians provide us no evidence that Marcus was ever vindictive, petty, cruel, or out of control. His reign was free of scandals, of shameful acts, of corruption. Isn't that a pretty low bar? Not when you compare it to the sickening and brutal list of crimes and disasters put together by his predecessors and successors, right on down to today, where it seems that the hardest thing to find in the world is an honest and decent person in a position of significant leadership.

Although Marcus was of good character, he knew that character was something that needs to be constantly worked on, constantly improved. He understood the second we stop trying to get better is the moment we start gradually getting worse. After the passing of Antoninus, he maintained his lifelong study of philosophy, humbly gathering up his tablets and going to school even as an old man. He never wanted to stop learning, never wanted to stop getting better.

What was he after? What was this destiny he sought?

It was, of course, an impossible ideal, but the work of his life was movement toward the place where he would be "never swayed by pleasure or pain, purposeful when in action, free from dishonesty or dissimulation, and never dependent on action or inaction from anyone else." Or, as he described it elsewhere, "self-reliance and indisputable immunity to the dice rolls of fortune."

That would be nice, wouldn't it?

In a sense, that's what temperance is: self-sufficiency. Purpose. Clarity. Power.

There's only one way to get there . . . and it's not through epiphany.

Speaking of her late husband, Mr. Rogers, Joanne Rogers remarked that "If you make him out to be a saint, people might not know how hard he worked." Antoninus and Marcus Aurelius are not dusty old parables from the past. They are not two-dimensional figures printed on the pages of history books. They were human beings. And they were not perfect. But if they were perfect, they would not give us hope.

We love them because they tried. Because they course corrected in failure, because they were humble in victory, because they did the work and got the results. This is what produces the path for us. Just as the living example and the loving instruction of Antoninus helped mold Marcus Aurelius, so, too, can the lives and lessons of Antoninus and Marcus Aurelius mold us.

We do not have to add our names to the list of sad stories and cautionary tales that success so often writes. Through self-discipline we can find our destiny: access to a higher plane of consciousness and being and excellence.

Antoninus found it, and the path he carved showed the way for Marcus.

Will we follow in their footsteps? Will we admire these heroes? Or will we go the way of the Neros?

That is the question we must ask ourselves now.

Tolerant with Others.
Strict with Yourself.

~

Cato the Younger was just as strict as his great-grandfather. He was indifferent to wealth. He wore ordinary clothing, and walked around Rome barefoot and bareheaded. In the army, he slept on the ground with his troops. He never lied. He never went easy on himself.

It came to be an expression in Rome: *We can't all be Catos.*

No one illustrated the impossibility of Cato's standards like Cato's own brother, Caepio. He loved luxury and favored perfumes and kept company that Cato never would have allowed himself. And yet Cato was humble enough in his own temperance to remember that it's called *self*-discipline for a reason.

While we hold ourselves to the highest standards—and hope that our good behavior is contagious—we cannot expect everyone else to be like us. It's not fair, nor is it possible.

Perhaps it was a rule articulated by Cato's great-grandfather that helped Cato love and support his brother despite their different approaches to life. "I am prepared to forgive everybody's mistakes," Cato the Elder said, "except my own." Ben Franklin, many generations later, would put forth an even better rule: "Search others for their virtues, thyself for thy vices." Or as Marcus Aurelius put it, *Tolerant with others, strict with yourself.*

The only person you get to be truly hard on is you. It will take every ounce of your self-control to enforce that—not because it's hard to be hard on yourself, but because it's so hard to let people get away with things you'd never allow in yourself. To let them do things you know are bad for them, to let them slack off when you see so much more in them.

But you have to. Because their life is not in your control.

Because you'll burn yourself out if you can't get to a place where you live and let live.

Credit them for trying. Credit them for context. Forgive. Forget. Help them get better, if they're open to the help.

Not everyone has trained like you have. Not everyone has the knowledge you have. Not everyone has the willpower or the commitment you have. Not everyone signed up for this kind of life either!

Which is why you need to be tolerant, even generous with people. Anything else is unfair. It's also counterproductive.

In 1996, the New Jersey Nets were trying to draft a young future superstar named Kobe Bryant. After an in-person workout, the team had to put him on a plane to the West Coast. The team, which then had a lean and efficient culture, booked him a middle seat in coach for the six-hour cross-country flight. Kobe wouldn't forget it. A moment of cheapness cost the Nets a shot at one of the greatest basketball players in history.

As it happens, Kobe himself would struggle his entire career with some version of this problem. He was one of the most exacting and dedicated players to ever step on a basketball court. But he had trouble accepting that his teammates "couldn't all be Kobes." In fact, many of them did not *want* to be Kobes. As he tried to drive them as hard as he drove himself, he often drove them into the dirt, or in other cases, like with Shaquille O'Neal, *drove them away,* depriving himself of a talented supporting cast that in the end could have earned him another ring or two . . . at least.

We talked earlier about keeping your cool. It's almost certain that the number one cause of angry outbursts from successful or talented people is the way that other people don't measure up. Why can't they get such simple things right? Why can't they just do it like we showed them the first time? *Why can't they just be like us?*

Because they are not us!

And even if they were, is it fair to expect something of them that they never signed up for?

Gandhi's friends always appreciated the grace he gave them, not judging them for their choices or for the less-strict lives they led.* "Dost thou think that because thou art virtuous," Sir Toby

---

* The only people he was too hard on were his children.

asks in Shakespeare's *Twelfth Night*, "there shall be no more cakes and ale?" Let them have their fun. Let them live and work as they please. You've got enough to worry about when it comes to your own destiny. It's not on you to try to change everyone else.

Be a strong, inspiring example and let that be enough . . . and even then try to be empathetic. In the run-up to the Gulf War, Colin Powell kept the fact that he was sleeping in his office a complete secret from his staff. The burden fell on his shoulders, not theirs, and he did not want them to feel like they had to try—even if they could—to match him sacrifice for sacrifice.

One of Lincoln's secretaries would marvel at the way the president "never asked perfection of anyone, he did not even insist, for others, upon the high standards he set for himself."

While good discipline is contagious, we can also be strong enough to accept that we are the only one who must live with such a severe case of it.

Discipline is *our* destiny. From Antoninus, Marcus Aurelius learned that just trying to escape our own faults is hard enough work to keep us busy for a lifetime. None of us are so perfect that we can afford to spend much time questioning other people's courage, nitpicking their habits, trying to push them to reach their potential. Not when we have so much further to go ourselves.

Understanding this should not just make us less harsh, but also *more understanding*.

Both Queen Elizabeth and her husband, Philip, struggled with this when it came to their children as well as with their siblings. Both were strict with themselves and believers in duty—so much so that it might have turned off their children to the concept.

Better to follow the model of Cato and Marcus Aurelius. Cato didn't lord himself over his brother, he loved him. With his step-brother, Lucius Verus, Marcus didn't hold his nose. He found things to love and appreciate in him—things that Marcus didn't have himself. And of his weaknesses? Marcus used his brother's vices to improve himself. Both were made better by being in each other's lives, both were enriched by the common ground and affection they found in each other.

This is the higher plane: When our self-discipline can be complemented by compassion, by kindness, understanding, *love.*

The fruit of temperance should not be loneliness and isolation. That would be a bitter fruit, indeed. Superiority is not a weapon you wield on other people. In fact, we have a word for that kind of intemperance: egotism.

Other people will choose to live differently. They may attack us for our choices—out of insecurity or ignorance. They may well be rewarded for things we find abhorrent or ill-disciplined. *And?* That's for them to deal with, and for us to ignore.

The journey we are on here is one of *self*-actualization. We leave other people's mistakes to their makers, we don't try to make everyone like us. Imagine if we were successful—not only would the world be boring, but there would be so many fewer people to learn from!

The better we get at this, the kinder we should become, and the more willing to look the other way.

We're on our own journey and, yes, it is a strict and difficult one.

But we understand that others are on their own path, doing the best they can, making the most of what they have been given.

It's not our place to judge. It is our place to cheer them on and accept them.

Make Others Better

~

Queen Elizabeth's father was, like Antoninus, not originally selected for greatness. He became king only by accident—due to the abdication of his brother in a fit of passion. Yet his impact on history would be enormous. It wasn't simply that he led Britain through a terrible war alongside Churchill but also because of the impact he had on the people around him.

In conquering a crippling stutter, George would inspire generations of young people struggling with that difficulty. But more ordinarily—in a way that every single parent can—he achieved immortality and lasting influence through his daughter. While his power was constrained by the constitution and cancer struck him down at age fifty-six, his example loomed large over young Elizabeth not just during his lifetime but every day since, as she asks herself, "What would my father have done?"

The same was true for Cato the Younger, who in everything he did, everything he tried to be was to live up to the example, to honor the legacy of his great-grandfather, that strict and austere Stoic, who he never even met. The same would go for countless generations since who would look to both Catos as heroes.

Some one hundred years after Cato's death, Seneca would advise that we all "Choose ourselves a Cato," a ruler to measure ourselves against. A model to inspire us to be what we're capable of being. When Nero's goons came to kill Seneca, he drew on Cato's example for strength in the last moments of his life. Some 1,700 years after that, George Washington would model his entire life on Cato's example, choosing his famous mantra from the mouth of his hero.

The two men had never met Cato . . . but he made them stronger. His discipline stiffened their spine when it counted.

Cato and King George VI then, by being so strict with themselves, actually had the effect that many leaders who are strict with their followers fail to achieve: They made people better.

To reach your destiny will require such a hero. But to truly fulfill it, you will need to become such a hero yourself—to live in such a way that you call others to reach their own.

Is this not what made Antoninus so great? His example, his faithfulness, his piousness, it served him well. It was good for its own sake, but it also molded and shaped Marcus Aurelius. Antoninus did not have to be strict with his young charge. His strictness was contagious—as were all his other virtues.

As Longfellow wrote about Florence Nightingale and indeed

all truly disciplined and wonderful people, "by their overflow / Raise us from what is low." Think about Churchill in those dark days of World War II—his courage, his self-control, his coolness under pressure, it helped his country find theirs.

That's what great leaders do: They make people better. They help them become what they are.

As it is written in the Bhagavad Gita, "The path that a great man follows becomes a guide to the world."

The self-disciplined don't berate. They don't ask for anything. They just do *their* job. They don't shame either . . . except perhaps subtly by their own actions. In their presence we feel *called* to step up, to step forward, to reach deeper because they have shown that is possible.

"Happy is the man who can make others better, not merely when he is in their company, but even when he is in their thoughts," Seneca wrote, speaking not only of Cato but all the men and women who inspired him.

That's the power of discipline. It makes you better . . . and then better still because of the positive effect it has on the world around you.

We don't all have to be Catos—again, the expression implies that we can't.

But we can be a positive force in our community. We can show our children, our neighbors, our colleagues, our employees what good choices look like. We can show what commitment looks like by showing up each day. We can show what it means to resist provocation or temptation. We can show how to endure. We can show how to be patient.

Maybe they'll appreciate this now. Maybe they'll hate us for it now. Maybe we'll be celebrated, maybe we'll be hated. We don't control that.

What's up to us is that we are good. That we do right. That we conquer ourselves. We can't force anyone else to do the same. But we can plant a seed. We can rest comfortably in our destiny, knowing that, eventually, inevitably, it'll make a difference for someone. Because like courage, there is something contagious about discipline.

The fire within us can burn bright enough to warm others. The light within us can illuminate the path for others. What we accomplish can make things possible for others.

It starts with us, it starts *within* us.

But it doesn't stop there.

Our discipline can be contagious . . . and if it isn't, how strong is it, really?*

---

* Certainly Queen Elizabeth's failures with her own children and extended family is a mark against her, just as Marcus Aurelius's failures with his son Commodus reflects poorly.

Grace Under Pressure

～

Hemingway was once asked for his definition of courage. He didn't say rushing into battle. Or slaying wild beasts. It wasn't staring down powerful interests, though his definition didn't preclude these things.

Grace under pressure.

That was his phrase.

Poise. Discipline when it counts.

The Queen has been calm and controlled as her life was threatened, as objects fell from the sky or the media besieged her palaces. But to her, this was all part of the job. After the 7/7 terrorist attack in 2005, in which fifty-two people were killed in the London subway system, she explained why this equanimity matters—that it was a *statement of character.* "I want to express my admiration for the people of our capital city," she said to the grieving yet resilient British people, "who in the aftermath of yesterday's bombings are calmly determined to resume their normal lives. *That* is the answer to this outrage." In an address in the early days of the pandemic, she would return to the same themes. "I hope in the years to come, everyone will be able to take pride in how they responded to this challenge," she said, "and those who come after us will say that the Britons of this generation were as strong as any. That the attributes of self-discipline, of quiet good-humored resolve, and of fellow-feeling still characterize this country."

In the year 175, Marcus Aurelius was betrayed by his general Avidius Cassius in an attempted coup. As always, Marcus responded with poise, even as he and his family were in mortal danger. "The nearer a man is to a calm mind," he wrote of such moments of crisis, "the closer he is to strength." A real man doesn't give way to rage or panic, he reminded himself, willing himself to be like Antoninus. "Such a person has strength, courage and endurance," he would say, "unlike the angry and complaining."

This doesn't just happen, as you know. It is the culmination of years of study and practice, of falling and getting back up, of getting better each day. "In my own case," Napoleon would say, "it's taken me years to cultivate the self-control to prevent my emotions from betraying myself." Napoleon may have been an ambitious megalomaniac, but no one could deny his poise on the battlefield.

Conversely, the samurai Musashi's genius was his ability to disrupt the poise of his opponents. He'd use any and every trick in the book to shake them, to break their concentration, and to make them upset. Once he did? They were beatable.

Grace under pressure looks beautiful, but it is a function of magisterial self-control and will. Of course the person is scared. They are tired. They are provoked. But they manage to subsume all that. They rise above it.

There is no leader, no artist, no parent who has made it their whole lives without high-pressure situations, without moments when it felt like things were spinning out of control, without a singular moment, in many cases, where *everything rested on what they did next.*

This is where they show who they are. This is where their destiny is realized.

We are told the story of a Roman knight named Pastor whose young and popular son was sent to prison by Caligula for some manufactured offense. Pastor attempted to intervene on his son's behalf, and so for the cruel spite of it, Caligula ordered the boy's execution.

To torture him further, Caligula then asked the man to dinner the night of his son's death—an invitation the man could not refuse.

What did Pastor do? What *could* he do?

He showed up.

But he refused to betray even a hint of his suffering or rage. Caligula toasted to his health and the man drained his cup to the last drop. The emperor passed down some gifts and he accepted them. We can imagine Pastor sitting there, surrounded as he was by laughter and people, feeling the loneliest and saddest and angriest man in the world. Yet he shed no tears, uttered no harsh words, and otherwise acted as if his beloved boy had been spared from this act of capricious cruelty.

How could he do this? To endure a loss is one thing. But to stand there as the knife is twisted, twisted for the pleasure of a cruel, deranged monster? To keep down food at the table of a murderer, to drink with perfect self-control when you want to retch and scream? Who could stand it?

Had he just gone numb? Was Pastor an unfeeling brute? Was he broken in spirit, bereft of courage?

No, the answer is much simpler than all that: *He had another son.*

His poise could not fail him, lest he fail his children. And so he didn't. Drawing on unspeakable, incomprehensible strength and dignity, he made it through—he kept his family safe.

We need to understand that temperance is more than just being mild or calm in stressful situations. It's more than just putting up with the occasional criticism or keeping some of your urges in check.

Sometimes it's having the strength to *not* do the thing you want to do more than anything else in the world. It's holding back the most natural and understandable and forgivable feelings in the world: taking it personally. Running away. Breaking down. Locking up with fear. Celebrating with joy. Cursing in anger. Exacting retribution.

To indulge these passions would be to give your opponents exactly what they want, or worse, to harm an innocent person.

A coup? A hostile interview? A game on the line with millions watching? A painful lie? A dangerous, life-threatening situation? A career-altering bet where all your chips get pushed to the center? For the people we love, we are strong enough to get through anything. For the cause or the calling we have committed to, we are strong enough to endure it. We have to be.

We can swallow our pain, as Pastor had to. We can gather ourselves up as Marcus did, as the Queen has done over and over again.

We do it because they're watching—our kids, our followers, our students, the world at large. We not only don't want to let them down, we want to inspire them, we want to show them what's possible, we want to show them that we really *believe* in this stuff.

"It doesn't matter what you bear," Seneca would say. "It matters how you bear it."

The truly great bear it with grace.

Poise.

Courage.

Discipline.

Carry the Load for Others

~

On Christmas Day 1998, General Charles C. Krulak arrived at Marine Corps Base Quantico expecting to find an enlisted man on duty at the guard station. He was surprised not to find him. He was even more surprised to find Brigadier General Jim Mattis working the post.

Had something happened?

No, but the man who was assigned guard duty that day had a family and Mattis thought he ought to be home with them. Despite some twenty years of seniority and the million other things he could have been doing with that time, Mattis chose to take over the unpleasant duties of an ordinary soldier.

A leader must be selfless, they must sacrifice, they must face the same deprivations as everyone else in the organization. If you can do this, Mattis learned from the writings of General Viscount Slim, "they will follow you to the end of the world."

"The privilege of command is command," Mattis once told a lieutenant he'd caught shirking. "You don't get a bigger tent."

In fact, the best commanders take the smaller tent. They pass their extra provisions on to their troops. They don't go easier on themselves, they go harder. Because they know that it's not just about them anymore.

"We are not on the level," a foot soldier once complained to Xenophon as he led the Ten Thousand Greeks out of Persia. "You are riding on horseback while I am wearing myself out with a shield to carry." Hearing this, Xenophon jumped down and carried the man's shield the rest of the way.

Being the "boss" is a job. Being a "leader" is something you earn. You get elevated to that plane by your self-discipline. By moments of sacrifice like this, when you take the hit or the responsibility on behalf of someone else.

Success does not free you from self-control, as we have said. It does not free you from hard work or consequences either. Now you will have to help others carry their loads too. And you will do this gladly, because when you accepted the rewards you also accepted the responsibility.

Gregg Popovich took the fine and the criticism so his players could have longer careers, and so other coaches in the future would benefit from this now-common practice. Harry Belafonte paid the bills so the King family could have a little peace of mind, a little rest.

When Antoninus took the throne, he reminded his wife that they would now have to be *more* generous. They would need to be stricter with themselves as well, more in control of themselves. "Now that we have gained an empire," he said, "we have lost even what we had before."

It'd be wonderful if power or success exempted us . . . from everything time-consuming, pedestrian, inconvenient, difficult. In practice, it obligates us to those things even more. It demands more of us. That's just how it shakes out.

Can you handle that?

The leader shows up first and leaves last. The leader works hardest. The leader puts others before themselves. The leader takes the hit.

Everything else is just semantics and titles.

As self-evident as this seems, it's sadly not the norm. For every Marcus Aurelius who sells the palace furnishings during a plague, there are senators who head for warmer weather while their constituents freeze in their homes without power or water. For every CEO who gave up their salary during the pandemic, there were companies that took government bailouts and then laid people off . . . and then gave bonuses to their executives. For every person who sacrificed for the sake of public health during the pandemic, there were prime ministers who threw parties and governors who treated themselves to large dinners at the French Laundry.

Too many leaders, Plutarch laments, think that the "greatest benefit in governing is the freedom from being governed themselves."

Nah, you're the one who has to follow the rules to the letter.

You're the one who has to show you really mean it. The more you've done, the higher the standard you must hold yourself to. The more you have, the more selfless you must be.

Not for the sake of optics, but because it is the *right thing to do*. Because that's what you signed up for when you took the responsibility.

Everything that General Mattis told his troops about sacrifice, about helping each other out, about duty, about humility, about empathy? None of it would have mattered as much as it did had he not been caught, time and again, actually *living* by those ideals.

We have to show, not tell: first in line for danger, last in line for rewards. First in line for duty, last in line for recognition. To lead, you have to bleed. Figuratively speaking. But sometimes also literally.

Is it really unfair? Or is it what you signed up for? And by the way, isn't it also what you get paid the big bucks for?

That's the privilege of command.

Be Kind to Yourself

Cleanthes was normally one to mind his own business. But as the Stoic philosopher walked through the streets of Athens one morning, he came upon a man berating himself for some failure. He couldn't help but say something, stopping to intervene with this upset stranger. "Remember," he said kindly, "you're not talking to a bad man."

Of course, the entire point of self-discipline is that we are strict. We hold ourselves to high standards. We don't accept excuses. We push ourselves always to be better.

But does that mean that we whip ourselves? That we hate ourselves? That we treat ourselves or talk to ourselves like a bad person?

Absolutely not.

Yet we slip, unconsciously, into these negative conversations all the time. *You suck. You screwed up. You blew it.*

You think the Dalai Lama walks around treating himself like that?

You blew it. So? You are not perfect. You are not superhuman.

No one is. The writer Ta-Nehisi Coates reminds us that "not all of us can always be Jackie Robinson—not even Jackie Robinson was always Jackie Robinson." The same goes for Cato, for Martin Luther King Jr., for Toni Morrison, for Queen Elizabeth.

And for Marcus Aurelius, too, who reminded himself and all of us not to "feel exasperated, or defeated, or despondent because your days aren't packed with wise and moral actions. But to get back up when you fail, to celebrate behaving like a human—however imperfectly—and fully embrace the pursuit that you've embarked on."

Failure is inevitable. Mistakes are bound to happen.

Everyone you have ever admired has lost their temper. They have hit the snooze button. They have fallen prey to bad habits. They have not been perfect spouses or neighbors or parents.

What would you have done if you had witnessed some of those moments? You would't have written them off or berated them. You'd have reassured them. You'd have reminded them of all the good they were doing, how incredible the feats they'd already accomplished were. You'd urge them to get back out there and keep going.

Now, can you tell that to yourself? Can you see *yourself* in that calm and mild light of philosophy?

Or are you too driven, too high-strung, too harsh?

"It is hard to have a Southern overseer," Thoreau wrote in *Walden* with some hyperbole, "it is worse to have a Northern one; but worst of all when you are the slave-driver of yourself."

Nobody likes tyranny . . . why would you be a tyrant to yourself?

Stoicism is not about punishing yourself. It's a firm school, for sure, but as Seneca wrote, "In fact no philosophical school is kindlier and gentler, nor more loving of humankind and more attentive to our common good to the degree that its very purpose is to be useful, bring assistance, and consider the interests not only of itself . . . but of all people."

And all people includes *yourself*, in case you need reminding.

After a lifetime of studying philosophy, this is ultimately how Seneca came to judge his own growth. "What progress have I made?" he wrote. "I have begun to be a friend to myself."

A friend to yourself.

You are not the enemy. You're the person doing the best you can. You're the person getting better every day.

You'd never let a friend say they were worthless. You'd never let them give up because it was too late. You'd never let them write themselves off. You'd refuse to let them abuse themselves, to torture themselves.

With a friend, we are able to remain calm. We are able to reassure. We give advice, not admonishments. This isn't just a kindness, it's also immensely helpful. We're able to be a resource for them, we're able to pull them out of the depths and get them back on the road to success and happiness.

Now imagine what you'd be capable of if you could regularly provide that service to yourself.

From a place of love and support, we grow.

It is an act of *self*-discipline to be kind to the self. To be a good friend.

Don't beat yourself up. *Build* yourself up. Make yourself better. That's what friends do.

The Power of Giving Power Away

George Washington finished the job and headed home.

He had just vanquished the British Empire, a whole continent now stretched before him as his spoils, and yet here he was, not only resigning his commission, but effectively turning down whatever power he might have asked for, whatever honor he could have dreamed up for himself. He could have named himself king and ensured his family ruled for centuries.

Instead, he bowed and handed in his sword.

Told of this plan, King George III was incredulous. "If he does that," he told the American painter Benjamin West, "he will be the greatest man in the world."*

Like Napoleon, Washington had studied the conquerors of history as a young man. He, too, had seen the cautionary tales of Alexander the Great and Julius Caesar. He just actually took

---

* Actually what made Washington the greatest (though still flawed) of the founders was his decision to free all his slaves, to give up his power over them, and do the right thing—the only one of his peers to do so.

their examples to heart. More, he was inspired by the story of Cincinnatus, the Roman statesman who, called upon in a terrible crisis, was given nearly unlimited power, only to relinquish it after saving his county and then returning to his quiet farm.

Managing our ambition is one thing. Holding ourselves accountable, another still. But turning down power? Willingly giving away or sharing the force that is supposed to corrupt absolutely?

It is the rarest thing in the world.

It is temperance embodied.

We are conditioned to acquire and acquire and acquire. We are told to fight our way to the top. Some of us are lucky enough to get there.

Head coach. CEO. Owner. President. Captain.

Why would you give it away once you have it? Why would you share what's *yours*?

Well, the most compelling reasons are on display in the people who cannot do this.

The history of Rome—indeed, the history of humankind— is almost universally the story of people who were made *worse* by power. From Nero to Napoleon, Tiberius to Trump, power doesn't just corrupt, it reveals. It places unimaginable stress on a person and subjects them to unbelievable temptations. It breaks even the strongest.

Dov Charney founded American Apparel, a fashion company based on fair labor practices and ethical branding. But as success came and temptations swirled, he slowly, steadily betrayed those principles, clinging to control and power, even as the stress and scrutiny sucked the joy out of the job. Investors, advisors, employees—all counseled him to bring on competent operators to help solve difficult problems, but he could not do it.* He preferred lackeys and young women he could have power over to sharing power and empowering others. Before his intemperance finally led the company's board to remove him, he was offered a last alternative: He could resign as the CEO and become a creative consultant, retaining his stock options and a million-dollar-a-year salary. Instead, he chose to destroy it all rather than face the prospect of someone else having even the slightest control over what he had built.

One of the brilliant innovations of the American founders was the separation of powers. They understood that concentrated power was dangerous and that leadership was a burden best widely distributed. Washington understood that he was handing it back to the people to divvy up and assign as they saw fit. Most ambitious leaders could not ignore the siren song . . . Washington could.

The person who cannot resist is a danger to themselves and to the organization. The person who *needs* this, who cannot bear to be anything but in charge, they are not great, even if they achieve great things. They are an addict! They do not have power,

---

*I myself gave this warning many times.

power has them. These are never the leaders whose organizations achieve sustained success or reach their potential because they are incapable of planning for their succession, they are incapable of empowering others, they are incapable of doing anything that diminishes their own significance.

Looking at the opportunities before him in the mild light of calm philosophy, Washington chose the path of Cincinnatus, back to Mount Vernon. He wanted quiet time alone. He wanted to humble himself with hard labor. He was observing the separation of civilian and military power. He was putting the country above himself.

It couldn't have been easy for an ambitious man with strong opinions about how things should go. Yet he did it.

But didn't Washington eventually become president? Yes, he did, reluctantly . . . and only after submitting to two popular elections. Then he resigned for the final time after two terms, setting an extra-constitutional norm of restraint that would be observed, unbroken, for the next 150 years before it was enshrined in the Constitution as the Twenty-Second Amendment in 1951.

In Rome, the emperor had incredible power—nearly anything they wanted was theirs if they asked. Yet both Marcus Aurelius and Antoninus chose to defer to the people's vote for the office of consul during their terms, running as private individuals instead of demanding the honor and power as a right.

If I were them, you might be thinking, *I would have taken the money. I would have seized the power.* And perhaps they would have, too . . . if they were you.

Plato said that the best leaders didn't want power. In truth, it's that they didn't *need* it. Because they have conquered their appetites and their ego, they are stronger, more independent, less corruptible, calmer, kinder, more focused on what matters.

After the war, Churchill was offered a dukedom by Queen Elizabeth. He was so moved and honored that he nearly broke down in tears. Then he caught himself and politely declined. "I remembered that I must die as I have always been," he said, "Winston Churchill."

What matters isn't the title. It isn't the power. It isn't the wealth. It isn't the control.

That greatness isn't what you have.

It's who you choose to become. Or who you choose to remain.

Turn the Other Cheek

~

At the Southern Christian Leadership Conference in 1962 in Birmingham, Martin Luther King Jr. stood before a large, integrated audience and gave the closing address. As King spoke, thanking the audience and reminding them of plans for the next year, a white man named Roy James walked onto the stage and began to savagely beat him.

The first punch struck King with such force in the face that he spun around. The next blows came in rapid succession, landing on his head and back, filling the now-silent auditorium with the sickening sound of bone connecting with flesh.

Septima Clark, in the audience, was stunned by this sudden burst of violence, not sure, at first, if it was part of a demonstration. But then she watched as King, gathering himself after the first onslaught, turned to face his assailant and drop his hands "like a newborn baby," to receive more blows. As he was being beaten, in front of hundreds of people, he actually opened himself to his attacker, literally turning the other cheek, as the ultimate demonstration of the principles of nonviolence and Christian love.

The display momentarily stunned James, too, just long enough for people to jump between them. "Don't touch him!" King shouted to the now furious crowd. "Don't touch him. We have to pray for him." As the crowd began to pray and sing, King spoke kindly to the man who had just beaten him, reassuring James that he would not be hurt before leading him to a private office where they talked. Returning to the stage sometime later, after taking two aspirin from Rosa Parks, King concluded the conference with an ice pack held to his face.

It is one thing to "take nonviolence as my lawfully wedded wife," as King liked to say, to try to ignore taunts and provocations. It's another thing to do this while you're being beaten by a Nazi in front of your closest friends and supporters.* It's another still to step *toward* the violence to show those friends and supporters what self-mastery looks like in the literal clinch, and to be forgiving enough to surprise even the Birmingham police by refusing to press charges.

It might be possible to punch a person who is that compassionate, but it is impossible to *beat* them.

King knew that. He wore America down with his capacity for suffering. He awed America with his restraint.

Responding, fighting back—this is expected. Rising above these understandable, even self-preserving instincts takes discipline. To be above it entirely is true self-mastery.

---

*James was an actual member of the American Nazi Party.

To King, there was something beyond political expediency to nonviolence. There was something about it that *elevated* a person. It could take the most ordinary, even flawed person, and allow them to reach—at least in the moment of crisis or protest—a transcendent, heroic plane. Such was the power of love and grace and forgiveness.

Turning the other cheek is a spiritual principle—something rooted in the virtue of justice to be sure—but it is also an act of will. You have to *do it*, even though it hurts.

In 1952, Sandra Day O'Connor took a lawfully wedded vow to marry her husband, John Jay O'Connor. For nearly forty years, across overseas postings, political campaigns, and then the highest court in the land, she did as she promised, loving and cherishing, having and holding, for better or for worse. But in 1990, he was diagnosed with Alzheimer's, putting that notion of *in sickness and in health* to the very real test. At first, she would bring him to work with her each day so he would not be lonely. Sandra would ultimately give up her dream job—a job meant to be held for life—to take care of him, even as her beloved husband had trouble recognizing her.

In 2007, a news reporter broke that John O'Connor had fallen in love with another Alzheimer's patient, as victims of Alzheimer's sometimes tragically do, forgetting his wife and marriage entirely. Gathering herself up, O'Connor decided to use her considerable platform to draw attention to this merciless disease and cooperate with the story. "I'm happy it makes John happy," she would say with a brave face . . . even as it must have broken her heart.

That's what *commitment* looks like.

The thing about marriage, about relationships, about putting ourselves up and out there in public is that they open us up to being hurt. They make us vulnerable. Protecting ourself is easy— all we have to do is close back up. To make it more than *five decades* as O'Connor did requires a continual turning of the other cheek, of remaining vulnerable, of putting another person first, of forgiving and loving and accepting and cherishing.

Can you do that? Are you strong enough? Do you *love* enough?

The same goes for the causes we have committed to. We'll fall short of them and have to get back up. Our commitment will be tested beyond comprehension. We'll be asked to sacrifice . . . and then sacrifice some more.

But if we can do it, if we can keep showing up, keep giving, and keep striving to live up to those impossibly high standards? Well, according to Martin Luther King Jr., we reach the mountaintop.

We touch something special, something higher, something holy.

How to Make an Exit

⁓

The most impressive operation of World War II was not the invasion of D-Day. It was, in a sense, the *opposite* of it. The landing on the beaches of Normandy involved nearly one hundred sixty thousand Allied troops. Comparatively, the retreat at Dunkirk, almost exactly four years to the day, involved the evacuation of some three hundred forty thousand troops. It did not take years to plan, there were no rehearsals; it was done on the fly, with the help of countless civilians and soldiers who calmly, collectedly, stepped up and did what needed to be done.

The former gets all the glory, of course, but it wouldn't have been possible without the transcendent heroism and discipline of the latter. One was magnificent, but the other, they knew even at the time, was a *miracle*.

It was a defeat, unquestionably, and yet the order and discipline with which it was handled actually *inspired* Britain. Churchill would give, in the following days, his famous speech about fighting on to the end, on the beaches, in the air, in the fields, and in the streets. Why did England think they could do it? Because of what Churchill saw at Dunkirk, he knew. "Wars are not won by evacuations," he said. "But there was a victory inside this deliverance."

Sometimes we have to rush in.

Sometimes we have to hold our fire.

But often, the hardest thing is to go the other way.

Our instinct is to charge ahead. There is a part of us that feels like it would rather die than admit defeat, or worse, run away. In storybooks, in history books, retreat is the opposite of heroism, of courage, of discipline. Yet that is sometimes exactly what we must muster the poise and courage to do.

At the Battle of Delium, Socrates found himself in such a situation. We don't tend to see Socrates as a soldier, but he was—and a good one, at that. The Athenian lines had broken and the men were in flight. But Socrates maintained his self-discipline and, even as he fled, was sure not to drop his arms or shield. We're told he continued to fight even as he left the field of battle. Alcibiades, a student of Socrates whose life Socrates had saved, would be profoundly inspired by the sight of the philosopher battling his way to safety, not abandoning anyone or anything of value—least of all his dignity. "This sort of man who is never touched in war," he would later say, "those only are pursued who are running away headlong."

Charging ahead is always inspiring . . . but sometimes it takes a bigger man—and another level of discipline—to be able to maintain your dignity when you have to go the other way.

It would be wonderful if no battles were ever lost by the good guys, if fearlessness or hard work were always enough, but this is not reality. Sometimes you have to live to fight another day. The question is not when you will have to do this, but *how* you will respond to it when that day comes.

For the Greeks, retreat wasn't a shameful thing. It was how you retreated well mattered. The most grievous sin was *rhipsaspia*—losing your shield in the chaos of escaping—because that endangered the whole phalanx, placing your comrades in peril. A Spartan could return from a battle lost, but they dared not ever abandon anyone. That's what they meant when they said *Return with your shield or on it.*

When things look lost, some just give up—terrible things come from this collapse of will. Disorder and apathy compound the problem, prevent things from being salvaged, even inflict collateral damage on others. This is not the way, as Socrates and the heroes of Dunkirk both show us.

At the same time, there are others who refuse to give up, thinking that this stubbornness is a virtue. But it, too, is a vice. The person who can only go forward . . . who never backs up, who has no escape plan, who is not brave but reckless. They are not self-controlled, they are stuck in one gear. You don't win everything, every time—not in war, in life, or in business. A person who doesn't know how to disengage, to cut their losses, or to extricate themselves is a vulnerable person. A person who does not know how to lose will still lose . . . only more painfully so.

Lincoln found that his father was trapped by the logic of an old expression: "If you make a bad bargain, hug it the tighter." This inability to let go, to change tactic, to admit a mistake, the so-called sunk cost fallacy embodied? It doomed the man to decades of failure and struggle, throwing good money after bad as the saying goes.

We'd like to think we're different, but are we?

We keep on dumbly doing the same things we've always done . . . under the illusion it will someday bring about different results. We think it's a sign of character that we won't give in, when it may well be stupidity or weakness. Or we think that we can continue going forward forever, when in fact it is exactly this insatiability that often leads us right into the trap that the enemy laid for us.

Hope is important but it is not a strategy. Denial is not the same thing as determination. Delusion is destruction. Greed will get you in the end.

Consider the self-control of Rocky Marciano, who walked away from fighting, when he sensed his body was done. He was one of the rare boxers who got out before it was too late. He was offered *$1 million* in 1956 to come back and fight Floyd Patterson—more than *double* what he made in his sixth and final title defense against Archie Moore the previous year. But he knew his time was up. He valued his brain more than his ego or his pocketbook.

Remember, it was ultimately Gehrig who benched himself, before his performance began to harm the team, handling his exit from the game with great dignity and poise, even when the thing he loved most was taken from him. You have to be strong enough to do that. To know when the jig is up. To know when you have to call TOD.

There's a story about Dean Acheson, then an undersecretary in the Treasury Department during the Great Depression. He found himself in a serious disagreement with FDR over a monetary issue. Acheson told FDR that the law was very clear, but FDR told him he expected his lawyers to find a way around the law. After an intense argument, Acheson submitted a polite and gracious letter of resignation, and then attended the swearing-in ceremony of his replacement, where he thanked a stunned FDR for the opportunity. Not only would Acheson come back to serve during the war, but FDR held him up as an example. "Tell him to ask Dean Acheson how a gentlemen resigns," Roosevelt once replied to a staffer who had handed him a petulant letter of resignation.

Can you put your ego aside and accept defeat—or irreconcilable differences? Can you walk away when it's time? Even when it's so tempting not to? Can you keep it together even as everything is falling apart—when all eyes are watching, waiting, for *you* to fall apart alongside it?

You must pay your debts, own your mistakes, communicate your intentions. You must have a plan for what you're going to do after. Whether that's a next project, a new chapter, another charge.

Retreats, we must remember, are only temporary. They are buying us time until we can take the offensive and courageously attack again in pursuit of our victory.

Endure the Unendurable

~

In his room in Heiligenstadt in October 1802, Beethoven was at his lowest ebb. His health had been failing for years. He was plagued by fevers and dysentery. He was tortured by crippling headaches. His heart was broken after more than one failed love affair, repeatedly blocked from marriage by his lack of noble status. His genius was not yet fully appreciated. Critics buzzed about him, but the old guard was still in control of the music scene. The wars of Napoleon still ravaged his homeland.

It was in this dark moment that he considered ending it all.

"For six years now," he would cry out in a letter to his brothers, "I have been hopelessly afflicted, made worse by senseless doctors, for year to year deceived with hopes of improvement, finally compelled to face the prospect of a *lasting malady* (whose cure will take years or perhaps be impossible). Though born with a fiery, active temperament, even susceptible to the diversions of society, I was soon compelled to withdraw myself, to live alone. If at times I was soon compelled to forget all this, oh how hardly I was flung back by the doubly sad experience of my bad hearing. Yet it was impossible for me to say to people, 'Speak louder, shout, for I am deaf.'"

The fates had ganged up on Beethoven. His body failed him. Events had conspired to break him; indeed, they would have broken most people.

Yet he did not break.

Staring over the precipice into blackness, a future where his greatest gift would disappear, somehow despite all his pain and anguish, he mustered the strength to carry on. "It was only my art that held me back," he wrote. "Oh, it seemed impossible to me to leave this world before I had produced all that I felt capable of producing, and so I prolonged this wretched existence.... I hope my determination will remain firm to endure until it pleases the inexorable Parcae to break the thread. Perhaps I shall get better, perhaps not, I am ready."

Virtue sustained him despite the indescribable misery. "Thanks to it and my art," he wrote, "I did not end my life by suicide."

How lucky we are that he had the self-control to resist this nearly fatal fit of passion. Without it we would not have his Für Elise, Piano Concerto no. 5, eight of his nine symphonies, or hundreds and hundreds of other pieces.

Of course, all things in life require some form of endurance.

Patience. Toughness. Delayed gratification. All that. But what about life itself? "Sometimes," as Seneca would write from the perspective of his own crippling illnesses and then exile, "even to live is an act of courage." And discipline too.

Life is not fair. It is not kind. It demands from us not just a strength of body and mind but also of soul—what the ancients called *karteria*, or perseverance. Otherwise, we could not bear to soldier on. We could not survive the blows of fate, the ones intended to discourage us, to make us quit on ourselves and abandon our wits, our principles, our philosophy.

"Forbearance is the sum total of our human virtue," said preacher Witness Lee.

Not just weathering a storm or two, but something beyond that . . . as anyone who has had a bad year or decade or worse. But it is this, the struggling, who are beset by difficulties and pain and doubt, who refuse to give up, who refuse to stop trying. This is more than courage. They have conquered themselves in body and mind, even if those are precisely the things working so hard against them.

We must look to them as heroes.

The philosopher Sextus Empiricus defined endurance as "a virtue which makes us superior to the things which seem hard to bear." Paul Gallico, writing about his friend Lou Gehrig, tried to define the heroism of the man, and settled on "among other things, the capacity for quiet, uncomplaining suffering, the ability to take it and never to let on, never to let the world suspect you are taking it."*

Seneca was exiled for eight years. Florence Nightingale spent sixteen years in waiting, thwarted from her call. James Stockdale must have yearned for death countless times as he hung there, his arms bound behind his back, a rope lifting him from the floor, popping his shoulders out of their sockets.

Think of the Queen pushing through her *annus horribilis*. Anne Frank in her attic for twenty-five months, cheerfully writing in her journal. Stephen Hawking, forty years in a wheelchair from ALS. Marcus Aurelius, plagued by a lifelong stomach ailment, then wars and floods and an actual plague, reminding himself that nothing was unendurable (and that the only thing that wasn't, our mortality, eventually solves that problem for us).

Think of the mothers who pushed through postpartum. Think of the people who fought through cancer, through bankruptcy, through humiliating failure. Think of the addicts who battled withdrawals to bounce back from rock bottom. Think of the people who clawed their way out of generational poverty. Think of the slaves who survived the worst of what humans can do to one another.

---

*Let us not confuse this with *not* asking for help. As the artist Charlie Mackesy wrote beautifully, "Asking for help is not giving up, it is refusing to give up."

They kept going. They didn't quit. Still, as Maya Angelou wrote, *still they rose*. And in so doing, they ennobled and dignified their struggle with endurance and quiet fortitude.

They proved themselves greater than the adversity that befell them. They kept going.

So can you.

Don't despair. Don't give up.

Keep the faith.

Because one day, you will look back from the other side of this struggle . . . and be glad you did.

All of us will.

Be Best

By AD 66, Pompey had already earned the title *magnus,* making him, in fact and in name, *Pompey the Great.* He had reconquered Spain. He had served as Rome's consul, not once but twice. He had defeated Spartacus in the Third Servile War.

And now he was being sent to dispatch with the Cilician pirates who terrorized the Mediterranean. Before he left, he stopped for a private consultation with the Stoic philosopher Posidonius, one of the great minds of the ancient world.

Posidonius's advice might have seemed rather redundant. "Be the best and always superior to others," he had told the ambitious general, quoting a line from *The Odyssey.* But Posidonius wasn't talking about achieving more victories over the enemy, he was talking about conquering the self. Not honors, but *being honorable.*

Plutarch tells us about a far less famous general and statesman in Greece, many generations before Pompey. Despite his brilliance on and off the battlefield, Epaminondas was appointed to an insulting minor office in Thebes. In fact, it was *because* of his brilliance that he was put in charge of the city's sewers. Instead of being provoked or despairing at his irrelevance—a number of jealous and fearful rivals thought it would effectively end his career—Epaminondas took fully to his new job, declaring that it is not the office that brings distinction to the man, it is the man who brings distinction to the office. With hard work and earnestness, Plutarch wrote, "he proceeded to transform that insignificant office into a great and respected honor, even though previously it had involved nothing more than overseeing the clearing of dung and the diverting of water from the streets."

Best is the person who adds shine to their accomplishments with their discipline, not the other way around.

This is what Posidonius was trying to tell Pompey, although Pompey failed to fully realize it. In the end, it's not about what we do, it's about how we do it and, by extension, *who we are.*

Too often, we find people choosing to be great at their profession over being a great human being, believing that success or art or fame or power must be pursued to the exclusion of all else.

Does it have to be that way? Does being loved have to be at odds with being lovely?

Or can temperance, as Cicero claimed, be the fine polish on top of a great life?

Queen Elizabeth inherited the monarchy. Marcus Aurelius was selected for the purple as a boy. But it wasn't the throne that made either of them kingly, it was their behavior. They were what the ancients called *first citizens,* for their character as much as their rank. As Marcus said, his aim was never to be the most powerful king, never to conquer the most territory, or build the most beautiful buildings. Instead, he was after "perfection of character: to live your last day, every day, without frenzy or sloth or pretense." It just happens that wonderful external accomplishments, like those achieved by Elizabeth and Marcus, can come out of internal endeavor. They are not the goal, they are the byproduct.

Conquering the world is almost easy after we have fully conquered ourselves. Certainly fewer people have done the latter than the former.

This is what you find when you study the true masters of any profession. They don't care much about winning, about money, about fame, about most of the things that have come their way as a result of their success. Their journey has always been toward something bigger. They aren't running a race against the competition. They are in a battle with themselves.

Self-discipline has never been about punishment or deprivation. It is about becoming the best, the best that *you* are capable of becoming.

The battle to be the best has less to do with beating others and more to do with beating down those urges, those flaws, those selfish instincts that every human has. Michael Jordan conquered his desire to quit in the famous "flu game" during the 1997 NBA Finals. But a greater Finals moment came in 2021, when the Phoenix Suns coach Monty Williams, a man who life has not gone easy on, entered the locker room of the newly crowned champions that had just beaten his team. "I just wanted to come and congratulate you guys as a man and coach," Williams told the Bucks. "You guys deserved it. I'm thankful for the experience. You guys made me a better coach. You made us a better team. Congratulations."

There was never enough for Pompey, nothing sacred. His endless ambition—his insane love of glory, as Posidonius called it—would ally him with Caesar, setting in motion the destruction of the Republic he once loved. He would wake up to this Faustian bargain eventually, and fight valiantly to preserve Rome, but it would be too late. He would be defeated by Caesar's armies at Pharsalus in a day, losing everything that he had acquired and then, shortly thereafter, losing his life as well. His last words would quote another ancient playwright, Sophocles:

Whoever makes his journey to a tyrant's court.
Becomes his slave, although he went there a free man.

By chasing the wrong kind of "best"—fame, fortune, power, *winning*—Pompey had chained himself to the "worst."

It cost him everything. As it does for all of us, when we compromise, when we relax our discipline, when we make "exceptions" and do what is expedient instead of what we know is right.

History is replete with great conquerors. There are far fewer generals who were great people. Talented writers, groundbreaking scientists, incredible athletes, bold entrepreneurs—all these types are rare. Rarer still, and all the more impressive, are those who manage to achieve these feats without losing control of themselves, without becoming slaves to their ambition, to their careers, to their urges.

Who will you be?

What race are you running? Who are you trying to beat? And is it for the best?

Flexibility Is Strength

~

The danger for Musashi was real.

Not the danger from the sword, or at least not that danger, directly.

Like anyone who trained intensely at something, Musashi was at risk of rigidity, of becoming trapped in a certain style, a certain approach. This is the natural by-product of any kind of specialization.

When you practice doing something a certain way a thousand times and then a thousand times again, this becomes the way you expect it to go, the way perhaps you *need* it to go. You follow your routine, you set up your system, you develop your style, and you find freedom in it . . . but also, potentially, slavery.

As he approached true mastery, Musashi needed to break free of these self-imposed chains. He knew the potential cost—having beaten many of his most awesome opponents simply by disrupting their flow or throwing them off-balance, by arriving late, by acting strangely, by choosing, in one case, to fight with a long wooden oar instead of a sword to the complete befuddlement of the warrior trying to kill him.

Would he become a prisoner of his method or would he break through it and into what the great strategist Robert Greene generations later would describe as *formlessness?*

Musashi chose the latter. He studied art and poetry. He deliberately pushed himself out of his comfort zone. He refused to stop growing, he refused to lock himself into anything—reinventing, changing, constantly becoming a newer, better fighter as he aged.

"With weapons as with other things," he would write, "you should not make distinctions. It is wrong for either general or soldier to have a preference for one thing and to dislike another. When you put your life on the line, you want all your weapons to be of use," he said. Or rather, you want to *have as many weapons as possible.*

You know that expression, "When all you have is a hammer, everything looks like a nail"? That is a warning. It's about rigidity. It's about seeing yourself a certain way, seeing your job a certain way and the limitations inherent therein.

The tricky thing is that this is partly what temperance is about. We hold certain things as sacred. We set up systems. We develop a style. We develop an identity. And then we stick to it. While everyone else is like a feather in the wind, we hold fast.

Great. But that will not be enough.

What makes Tom Brady the greatest quarterback of all time

was one thing. It was another asset that contributed to his remarkable longevity, allowing him to add multiple championships to his haul, well into his forties. His commitment and hard work made him great early. But what allowed him to sustain his body is his *pliability*. Other players worked on getting stronger and bigger . . . Brady on flexibility. He's limber. He's light. But this pliability is figurative too. He doesn't *force* things to be a certain way—he adjusts, always, to how the game is changing, to new rules, to new receivers, and to a new team in a new city with a new generation of athletes.*

Now we're supposed to know how to change too?

Yup.

A colleague of Churchill once captured the balance perfectly when he observed that Churchill "venerated tradition but ridiculed convention." The past was important, but it was not a prison. The old ways—what the Romans called the *mos maiorum*—were important but not to be mistaken as perfect. Think of Queen Elizabeth . . . a protector of a timeless institution who somehow never allowed herself to fall out of step with the times. That's what the Beatles were talking about when they sang, "Her Majesty's a pretty nice girl / But she changes from day to day." And

---

* This would be the lesson the Los Angeles Rams learned losing the Super Bowl in 2019: They were too rigid and couldn't adapt. Coming back in 2022, Coach Sean McVay focused on relaxing, not overtraining, and getting to a place of *stillness*.

it's what she proved when she honored the Beatles with the MBE (Member of the Order of the British Empire) in 1965, a move that was intensely unpopular with traditionalists at the time, but, in retrospect, a very necessary step forward for the monarchy's involvement in British culture.

Of course, some things, like our principles, cannot change… but everything else? We have to be strong enough to adjust and adapt… lest we end up angry, bitter, and impossible to work with.

The college basketball coach Shaka Smart, upon moving from coaching at Texas to Marquette, in Milwaukee, Wisconsin, was asked if he was a cold-weather or warm-weather guy. "I'm a dress-for-the-weather guy," he said.

We must learn how to be flexible, to roll with the punches or the weather or the realities of the moment.

Our discipline cannot ossify into a set approach, as it so naturally is inclined to when it is working for us. It's not just success that does this to us, though. Anyone is susceptible, especially with age, to become set in their ways, even if those ways are not serving us well. Susan Cheever, writing about Thoreau, would paint a tragic picture. "As he aged and had absolutely no success in his chosen field, as his world crumbled around him," she wrote, "Thoreau seemed to become more and more rigid. All he had were his principles. Instead of believing in them, he seemed to be ruled by them." It was the definition of insanity—what wasn't working, he stuck to, trapped in an emotional and artistic ghetto of his own making.

It calls to mind a warning that a trainer once gave to Muhammad Ali, whose forceful will made him stand tall always. *An oak tree stands tall too*, the trainer told him, *but you have to bend and sway or be knocked down.* "Oak makes good coffins too," he reminded Ali.

Plenty of people have been buried in coffins of their own making. Before their time too.

Because they couldn't understand that "the way they'd always done things" wasn't working anymore. Or that "the way they were raised" wasn't acceptable anymore.

We must cultivate the capacity for change, for flexibility and adaptability. Continuously, constantly. Changing the little things day to day, as the Queen did, to preserve and protect the big things. It's not always fun. It's not always easy.

But what's the alternative? Dying?

Self-control is not a life sentence. It is a *way* of living.

Flexibility doesn't mean we throw out what's important, but it does mean understanding how to live and let live, how to rest comfortably in our traditions while allowing new and improved ones to be created. It also means, as the world changes and our position within it changes, adjusting, finding a way to be true to our principles that doesn't condemn us to bitterness or needless failure or being on the outside of things.

Rigidity is fragility. Formlessness is unbreakable.

We can choose one or the other.

Unchanged by Success

～

On the night the Berlin Wall fell, Angela Merkel had one beer and then went home. The crowds surged in an almost orgiastic frenzy of relief and excitement. She went to bed early. She had something she wanted to work on the following day.

Even after she was elected chancellor, a stunning rise to one of the most important offices in Europe, she continued to live in the same ordinary, rent-controlled apartment that she's been in for twenty-three years. When she attends concerts at the Philharmonic, she sits in regular seats (which she insists on paying for) alongside the rest of the audience. She's been known to chide aides she knows are laughing too hard at her jokes. And Berliners have long become accustomed to seeing the former "Leader of the Free World" shopping for her own groceries at the store.

A journalist once asked Merkel if it bothered her, after all she accomplished, that people in her hometown still referred to her as "the pastor's daughter." That's who I am, she replied. No matter what changes in her life, that will remain true.

The same went for Cato the Elder, whose early austerity made him stand out against Rome's decadent leaders. "What was even more remarkable," Plutarch wrote, "was that he followed the same habits, not merely when he was young and full of ambition, but even when he was old and gray headed and had served as a consul and celebrated a triumph, and that he continued, like a champion athlete, to observe the rules of his training to the end."

Such is the paradox of success. Precisely when we think we've earned the right to relax our discipline is exactly when we need it most. The payoff for all our efforts? So much more temptation. So many more distractions. So many more opportunities.

The only solution?

Even more self-mastery!

Achieving things is great. Becoming a selfish jerk because you accomplished them? Thinking you're suddenly better or matter more than anyone else? C'mon.

What impressed Plutarch about Cato and impresses us about Merkel is that they didn't use their power or position to purchase what so many people do—ego. Or exemptions from the rules.

One of the most moving photos of the funeral for Prince Philip is of tiny Queen Elizabeth, nearly ninety-five years old, sitting entirely alone in St. George's Chapel in mid-2021. Of course, the Royal Family had been offered the opportunity to invite more people to the funeral. It was a kindness that the

Queen immediately declined on the grounds that it would be unfair to the millions of Britons and citizens of the Commonwealth who had observed and respected the safety protocols during the pandemic.

After a lifetime of respecting protocol, she wasn't about to make an exception. She might have been able to escape the consequences . . . but not the dishonor. Yes, it meant she had to spend one of the toughest days of her life alone . . . and yet she was not unaided in this. Duty stiffened her spine. Discipline helped her through it. More, her monkish devotion *elevated* her.

"Lift me up and hurl me, wherever you will," Marcus Aurelius wrote in *Meditations*. "My spirit will be gracious to me there—gracious and satisfied." He meant this not just because he was a good friend to himself, but because the result of his moderation and self-control was resilience. The gift of his strictness, of his self-containment, was tranquility—amid both success and adversity. This is something we can all have when we stop caring what other people say or do, only *what we do*. When we focus only on heading "straight for the finish line, unswerving."

So it went for Merkel when she took the controversial step of allowing one million refugees into Germany—the most of any country in Europe during the Syrian crisis. She could have ignored the growing humanitarian nightmare. She could have made it some other leader's problem. She could have played it small, thinking only of her electoral chances at home, as most successful politicians do.

Instead, she approached it as a *pastor's daughter*, the person she was raised to be, not the politician she had become. She approached it as a human being. She did what she thought was right. She wasn't afraid. She didn't care if she was criticized. The only part of her that had been changed by her success was her ability to direct world events—and that power she seized.

It's easy to be modest when you have much to be modest about. But now you're in a position to indulge your passions. It's easy to follow the rules when you are not above rules. Now people will make excuses for you. Now it really is about *self*-discipline, because all the other forms have gone away.

It's at the height of our powers that we need the clearest mind. We can't be blinded by substances or a sense of superiority. "People of humble station have more leeway when it comes to using force, bringing suits, rushing into quarrels, and indulging their anger," Seneca wrote, for "blows traded by equals do little harm. But for a king, even raising his voice to use intemperate language is at odds with his majesty."

Self-mastery is one of those things that demands more of itself while not necessarily begetting more of itself at the same time. Not only does self-mastery not make itself any easier to achieve, but the rewards for it are a million seductive reasons (and dollars) to let up.

But you're going to show them that you're better and bigger than that. That your victory was not a fluke, but that you deserved it and have what it takes to build and maintain it.

You will concentrate your mind on what counts.

You will not be inflated by the changes in your fortune.

You will show that success has not changed you.

Except that it has made you *better*.

Self-Discipline Is Virtue.
Virtue Is Self-Discipline.

～

The virtues are like music. They vibrate at a higher, nobler
pitch.

STEVEN PRESSFIELD

I n the beginning," Goethe opens his play *Faust,* "was the Word."
Then he corrects himself. No, in the beginning there was
the *deed.*

This has been a book about self-discipline, the second in a
series about the cardinal virtues. Here at the end of it, it's worth
pointing out: Words don't matter. *Deeds do.*

Nothing proves this more, in fact, than the relationship between temperance and the other three virtues of courage, justice, and wisdom. These things are impossible, worthless even,
without self-discipline to bring them about.

Nearly every single one of the American founders—from
Washington to Franklin to Adams and Henry—made some ver-

sion of the argument that their novel system of government was *impossible without virtue* in the people. Mainly they were talking about the virtue of temperance, the idea that freedom could not be sustained unless tempered by private restraint. Indeed, a people without self-control, Adams said, would break "the strongest cords of our Constitution as a whale goes through a net."

We can fight courageously for our rights, for the power to be our own masters—as we are entitled to be—but that means, ultimately, we have to be responsible for ourselves. Because if we are not, someone or something else must be. See how far you get without self-discipline, how long your success lasts, how quickly any virtue can become a vice if taken too far . . . including courage, justice, and even wisdom.

Self-discipline is the only way. It's the moderating influence against the impulse of all other things.

"Supplement [courage] with self-control," Cicero wrote, "and then every ingredient for the happy life is yours. For you will have courage as your defense against distress and fear, and self-control to liberate you from sensuality and keep you free of immoderate cravings."

Talking about virtue is easy. It flowed well onto these pages, buttressed by centuries of poetry and literature and memories. But the purpose of writing this book, and the hours you spent reading it, was not mere entertainment. That's not what philosophy is about.

We are here trying to actually get better. Trying to answer our own call, to make that Herculean choice ourselves. Today. Tomorrow. At every moment.

What good will any virtue be if it exists only on paper? What's the point if you don't have the courage to live it? To stand alone with it? To insist on it even with so many rewards accruing to a life moving in the opposite direction?

Sure, there is a relationship between study and practice, but at some point the rubber meets the road. We contemplate truth and then we have to act on it.

The four virtues are about instilling character—good character—so that at the critical point, a person's true nature kicks in. Self-discipline is not something that just happens to you, it is something you cultivate. Just as a writer only becomes one by writing—and a great writer by writing that which is worth reading—*being* disciplined is something you prove by the life you lead.

The people we have followed so far, from Lou Gehrig to Marcus Aurelius, Queen Elizabeth, George Washington, Martha Graham, Harry Truman, Joyce Carol Oates, Booker T. Washington, Floyd Patterson—they were not perfect. At times, they exhibited the exact opposite of the virtues we are studying, and that must be noted. Still, it cannot be denied that at key, critical moments, their *character* kicked in and they did something profoundly great. Not just then, for the people they helped or the cause they furthered, but also today, for us, in the inspiration their achievements provide.

It wasn't their words that mattered. It was what they did because of who they were.

That's what Lincoln expressed at Gettysburg: It doesn't matter what we say here, it matters what *they did there.* Whether Lou Gehrig, the pride of the Yankees; or Marcus Aurelius, struggling to live up to his destiny and the example of Antoninus; or Queen Elizabeth, struggling under similar pressure some twenty centuries later; or Floyd Patterson, trying to claw back his title; or Beethoven, crawling back from the brink of suicide—their self-discipline, their temperament, their endurance calls down to us.

Their virtue shines.

We cannot consecrate it. It stands eternal on its own.

There is only one way we can honor it.

By adding to it our own deeds, by picking up their unfinished work. We must continue the tradition we are now a part of, whether we know it or not.

It begins by polishing our own virtue. Not with virtue signaling, but with virtuous *living.*

We can learn about virtue all we want, but when we get to the crossroads, there we will have to make a choice.

We opened this book with the Bible and with John Steinbeck. Let us close by bringing them together. In *East of Eden,*

Steinbeck concludes that the most powerful phrase in Christianity is *timshel*. When we read the commandments translated into English, they are rendered as just that, *commandments*. But Steinbeck thinks the Hebrew rendering is more accurate, not "Thou shalt" but "Thou mayest."

"Here is individual responsibility and the invention of conscience," he reflected to his editor as he wrote those pages. "You can if you will but it is up to you. This little story turns out to be one of the most profound in the world. I always felt it was, but now I know it is."

Whether it's from the Bible or from Hercules or *East of Eden* or *Faust,* the parable's message is the same: *We have a choice.* We *choose* between self-control and ill-discipline, virtue and vice.

Self-control must be observed physically. It must be embodied mentally. It must be rendered magisterially when our moment comes.

It's our decision what this will look like. Not just once, but a thousand times in life. Not just in the past and the future but right now, today.

What will it be?

Dependence or independence?

Greatness or ruin?

Discipline is destiny.

It decides.

Will you choose it?

Afterword

~

Two years into writing this book, I hit a wall.

To meet the aggressive deadlines set by my publisher, I knew that the writing would need to begin in early June. But as I sat in my office, looking through my piles of material, that seemed almost impossible. Almost always by the time I sit down to type the first sentence of a book, I know exactly what I am going to say on every page.

Like inspiration, "winging it" is for amateurs.

A pro has a plan.

Yet, terrifyingly, I did not have one. Of course, I knew the broad scope of the book, but too much was uncertain. Structure, characters, examples, all of it was beyond me. And how would I possibly make something as unsexy as temperance interesting to the reader? I did not know. Worse, I began to question whether I *would know*.

There is no other word than *despair* for what I was feeling. Doubt? One always has that. Dread? There is always a little bit of that before someone tries something difficult. This was deeper.

No, this was a crisis of confidence—that I had the wrong topic, I didn't have the material, and my moment had abandoned me. So there I was contemplating whether to call my publisher and ask for a delay.

I was also tired. Just so tired.

Coming up with the *idea* for a book is a creative pursuit. Actually *creating* the book is a work of excruciating manual labor, sitting in a chair, grinding out each consecutive sentence—a process not measured in hours or days, but months and years. It's a marathon of endurance, cognitive and physical.

For me, in the last decade, I have run not just a couple of these marathons but twelve of them, back to back to back. That's roughly 2.5 million words across titles I've published, articles I've written, and the daily emails that I produced in the same period. And on this book—the halfway mark in my series on the four virtues—it strikes me that we are well into the third calendar year of a destabilizing, devastating global pandemic, which I began with two children under four. I am sitting here in a nineteenth-century historic building, above a bookstore, which I also started and opened during the same roiling, uncertain period. This morning, like all mornings, I was up at seven, walking with the kids as we inspected the fences on the cattle ranch where we live.*

---

* I concede I could do a better job of keeping the main thing the main thing.

It was as if all this was catching up to me when I could least afford it.

I'm not someone inclined to believe in divine intervention. But I needed help . . .

On a sweltering-hot day in Texas, I was sitting at my workroom table, going through boxes that contained thousands of note cards of research. As a whole, they overwhelmed me—what they contained, the way they might fit together to produce a book, seemed impossible to comprehend. I reached out and grabbed one.

It had just two dozen words scrawled in red Sharpie. When was it written? Why had I written it? What had prompted me? All I know is what it said.

> Trust the process. Keep doing my cards. When I check them in June—if I have done my work—there will be a book there.

It wasn't exactly a miracle . . . but defying space and time, I had traveled from the past into the future to deliver a reminder of self-discipline.

And guess what? *It saved me.*

Not from the work, of course, but from myself. From giving up. From abandoning the system and process that had served me so well on all those books and articles and emails. In one of the best passages in *Meditations*, Marcus Aurelius, almost certainly in the depths of some personal crisis of faith, reminds himself to "Love the discipline you know, and let it support you."

That's what my note said to do.

So I listened.

I began showing up at the office earlier each day to work with my material. Card after card, I sorted them into tiny little piles. Looking for connections, for threads I could follow, for the key that would unlock the book.

Instead of worrying, I used the calm and mild light of the philosophy I have written about in my books. I went for long walks when I got stuck. I tried to follow my routine. I tuned out distraction. I focused. I also sat—just sat—and thought.

I trusted the process. I loved the discipline I knew. I let it support me.

I'd love to be able to tell you that shortly after this the book just *clicked*. But that's not how writing, or life, works. What actually happened was slower, more iterative, but also in the end, just as transformative.

As I walked that long hallway of despair, light began to creep in. Lou Gehrig stepped forward from the shadows. After nearly four thousand pages of biographies, Queen Elizabeth entered as a portrait of temperament. One character after another slowly, painstakingly, chapter by chapter, became discernable.

The book was there, as my note promised me. Now I had to write it.

One good thing about the pandemic is that it was a kind of forced lifestyle experiment, a chance to refine and improve my daily writing routine. As the days blurred together and the previously infinite opportunities of ordinary life disappeared, all that was left was the day—all that remained were the words I had to write.

I would wake early and dress the children. I'd strap them in the stroller and we'd walk or run as the sun came up and my wife caught up on much-needed sleep. We counted the deer lounging in the fields and watched the rabbits dart across the paths. We talked and we noticed things. We enjoyed one another's company—fully, completely, with no interruptions. My rule has long been that I don't check my phone for the first hour of the morning. It's not just about managing screen time, but making room for moments like that . . . and for the ideas that would magically pop in my head—like Beethoven's *raptus*—when work was the last thing I was thinking of.

When we got back to the house, I would set the kids up to play and take a shower. I work for myself, but it's important to *feel,* as opposed to look, fresh—so I shave each morning. My work means too much to me to show up like a slob. So I put on a simple set of clothes (roughly the same thing each day to reduce unnecessary choice) and then sit down with my journals. Whether it takes five minutes or twenty-five, it centers me. Anne Frank wrote (in her own journal) that paper is more patient than people. She was right—one of the best ways to temper difficult emotions is to do it on the page . . . and to leave it there.

After the journaling, then it was time to work—the most important, hardest thing first. I would pull up to my office at the bookstore, set my stuff down and write. No delays, no procrastination, no digital distractions. Just writing. Sometime during those tough early days of the book, I put a note card up on my wall with a quote from Martha Graham: "Never be afraid of material. The material knows when you are frightened and will not help." Self-discipline is pointless without courage, and, of course, the defining characteristic of courage is self-discipline—*steeling yourself* for what must be done.

While a book requires many, many hours of work, these hours come in rather small increments. If I get to the office at eight thirty, I could be done writing by eleven. Just a couple hours is all it takes. Just a couple crappy pages a day, as one old writing rule puts it. The discipline of writing is about showing up.

The seasons changed. World events raged and spun as they always do. Opportunities, distractions, temptations, they did what they do too—popping up, pinging, nagging, seducing. Day after day, I kept after it. To the right of my computer monitor, between two photos of my boys, is a picture given to me by the sports psychologist Jonathan Fader. It's the famed Dr. Oliver Sacks and behind him is a large sign he kept in his office that just said *NO!* By saying no—to interviews, to meetings, to "Can I pick your brain for a minute?"—I was saying yes to what matters: my family. My work. My sanity.

And work is more than just writing. There's always business to do and problems to solve. In the afternoon, I schedule my phone calls and interviews. I edit, read, record podcasts for *Daily Stoic* and *Daily Dad*. I work on projects for the bookstore and my other businesses. Still, no matter how busy the day, I am home for dinner each night—and ideally, in time to get lost in play with the kids before dinner too. In the evenings, we go for a walk again and then I put the kids to bed.

To me, nothing has required and strengthened my discipline more than having kids. I try to think about how hard it is to be little—especially in these uncertain times. I try to remember that rushing through things, whether it's bedtime or the drive to school, means rushing through time we have together, time we'll never have again. I catch myself when I get frustrated or provoked: The kids are just tired. They're hungry. They don't know how to communicate. As we lay in bed together, I say to myself, "This is wonderful. Nothing is better than this." It struck me in 2021, as I got on a plane for the first time in eighteen months, that I'd had five hundred consecutive nights at home. No wonder I had been so productive . . . no wonder I was so happy, as difficult as things were.

For myself and for my kids, I try to stay disciplined in all facets of my life. I eat healthy, usually fasting about sixteen hours a day.

Aware of my tendency to do things compulsively, I don't drink or smoke or take recreational drugs of any kind. I avoid the steady drumbeat of the increasingly negative news media, trying to remain positive and to keep up the good fight in a broken world. I keep my ego in check and, to the best of my ability, my temper too. I do my best to be a good husband and supportive spouse. I get my sleep. I keep my desk clean—or clean*ish*. I eliminate inessential tasks and delegate the ones that others can do.

During the writing of this book, I had lunch with Manu Ginóbili, the four-time NBA champion, an All-Star, and an Olympic Gold Medalist and, as it happens, one of the players whom Gregg Popovich rested in that controversial game back in 2012. Although champions like Michael Jordan and Tiger Woods are indisputably great, I'm much more impressed with world-class performers who find a way to live balanced and decent personal lives. As we sat on the back porch, I told Manu about some of my struggles, and he told me the story of the 2013 NBA Finals.

With five seconds left in Game 6, the Spurs had a three-point lead and Manu went up for the rebound that would close out the series. He was just barely outjumped by the much taller Chris Bosh, who passed the ball to Ray Allen, who sent the game into overtime with a clutch three. On the final play of overtime, the Spurs down by one, the ball was back in Manu's hands, as he drove to the basket. It was his moment. His shot.

And it was not to be. The ball was stripped away. The Heat won. The series went on to a Game 7, which the Heat won.

He told me that before that, he'd always taken losses hard. But after this one? His house felt like a funeral. It was filled with grief and anger and pain and despair. He was like Floyd Patterson after losing the belt. He couldn't eat or think. He was *miserable*.

There are a couple ways to go from that. Bitterness. Regret. Resignation. You could train harder, become more driven, take winning even more seriously. Instead, a thought struck him as he moped and ruminated: *I just played in the NBA Finals*, he said to himself, *how am I not having any fun?*

The following year, the Spurs were back. Following the devastating Game 7 loss, he and the Spurs came back to beat the Heat in just five games to win his fourth NBA championship, and the team's fifth.

But the biggest feat was how he changed his relationship to the game, to winning and losing. It wasn't anger or revenge that was driving him. He was actually enjoying himself.

He became more balanced, more in control of his emotions. He was more present. He had more fun. And he was a better father and husband and teammate as a result. Manu played five more NBA seasons after that heartbreaking loss (sixteen seasons in all), retiring as the Spurs' all-time leader in three-pointers and steals. He was third in games played, fourth in assists, and fifth in points. In 2019, the Spurs retired Manu's No. 20 jersey. He's now in the Hall of Fame.

This, too, is what temperance is about. When we say that self-discipline saves us, part of what it saves us from is ourselves. Sometimes that's from our laziness or our weakness. Just as often, it's from our ambitions, from our excesses, from our impulse to be too hard on others and ourselves. It makes us not just great at what we do, but *best*, in that fuller sense of the word. Aristotle, who wrote so much on the topic, reminded us that the point of virtue wasn't power or fame or money or success. It was *human flourishing*.

What is more important than that?

As I struggled to write this book, I tried my best to improve in another area of my life—how my work and self-discipline manifests itself at home. Several years ago, after I sold a project, my editor called my wife, in part to congratulate us but also to apologize. She knew what this meant for my wife—what it would do to me, who I became in the dark depths of writing a book.

However this book does, even if it makes a difference for a lot of people, what I am proudest of is *who I was while I wrote it*. There were fewer apologies necessary, even when it felt like it might not come together. Even that moment where I felt like I might need to delay the book, I remember thinking: *And?* So what? Sometimes things have to be delayed.

Festina lente.

As hard as a book can be to start, the end stages are toughest—it's usually a scramble, deadlines loom, and a million problems appear. It's not always been my finest hour. But then, as I worked from home on the final pages on this book, my five-year-old looked up from his art project and said, "I'm sorry you lost your job writing books, Dad." Apparently things had been so much less crazy and my boundaries had been so much better that he thought I'd been forced into early retirement.

A less disciplined me, a younger me? I would have been wrecked by the stress of an even less stressful book. I would have acted out. I would have been consumed. I would have carried it home. There was no calm and mild light for me when it came to my work. I was all ambition and drive . . . and when something got in the way, indomitable and aggressive. It helped me accomplish things. It also made me unhappy.

It would not have served me well on this project. Worse than that, it would have made me a hypocrite.

So yes, as I finish here, I am still tired.

I am *so* tired. I also feel wonderful.

Life is for the living. We are meant to be up and doing.

If books came naturally, without effort? Everyone would write them.

And for [books], you can plug in whatever it is that you do. It's good that it's hard. It's good that it can be discouraging. It's good that it breaks your heart, kicks your ass, messes with your head. But it can also be done with balance, with sustainability, and, most of all, with temperance.

That's what separates the disciplined from the undisciplined, the weak from the strong, the amateurs from the pros.

Nobody ever said destiny was going to be easy.

Would it be worth anything if it was?

What to Read Next?

For most people, bibliographies are boring. For those
who love to read, it's the best part. In the case of this book,
which relied on so many wonderful authors and thinkers,
I could not possibly fit the entire bibliography in the book.
Instead, I've prepared a full list not only of all the great books
that influenced the ideas you've just read, but also what I got
out of them and why you might like to read them. To get this
list, please just email books@disciplineisdestiny.com or go to
disciplineisdestiny.com/books. I'll also send you a list of some
great quotes about courage.

CAN I GET EVEN MORE BOOK RECOMMENDATIONS?

YES. You can also sign up for my list of monthly book
recommendations (now in its second decade) at
ryanholiday.net/readingnewsletter. The list has grown to
include more than two hundred thousand subscribers all
over the world and has recommended thousands of life-
changing books. I'll start you off with ten awesome books
I know you'll love.

Acknowledgments

~

As I approach the halfway point of this series, I must acknowledge the many people who helped me get here. My editors and marketing team at Portfolio and Profile, thank you. My agent, Stephen Hanselman. My team in Texas—Adrianna Hernandez, Jessica Davidson, Billy Oppenheimer, Justin Dumbeck, Dawson Carroll, Jane Brady Knight, as well as Nils Parker and Brent Underwood, make it possible for me to write. Same goes for my in-laws, Rod and Keran, who were our only childcare these last two years. There is this idea that "the pram in the hall" is the enemy of art. My boys have made me more disciplined and given me more focus than I ever had before. I can't imagine life without them. Most of all, I must thank my wife, Samantha, who has a much more effortless (and, frankly, happier and kinder) approach to daily discipline that I continue to learn from. She supports my crazy habits and routines along with tolerating the many hours (and dark nights of the soul) that have gone into producing all my books over the last ten years. And thank you to the many people in this book and in my life (Robert Greene, Marcus Aurelius, et al.) who have made me better by their example.

Also by Ryan Holiday

Also by Ryan Holiday and Stephen Hanselman

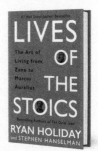

RyanHoliday.net
DailyStoic.com

Interested in learning
even more about Stoicism?

Visit

DailyStoic.com/email

to sign up for a daily email,
engage in discussion, get advice,
and more.